ELEPHANT GRASS

Elephant Grass

John Cowell

First Published in Great Britain in 2007
By
John Cowell,
C/O Cremer Press, Blackburn.

ISBN 978-1-897822-1-73-1

Printed and Bound By
Edmund Mercer, Cremer Press,
45 Harrison Street, Blackburn.
Lancashire, BB2 2JE.

4

ACKNOWLEDGEMENTS

I would like to thank all my friends and family who encouraged me to write my memoirs about my time spent in Africa during my National Service days. My gratitude is expressed personally to my friend Agnes Kershaw, my son Craig, my cousin Michael Walsh and my editor Madeleine Fish, all of whom painstakingly proof-read my book.

Many thanks to my friends, Martin Grogan and Howard Fanshaw from Burnley, Duggie Smith from Liverpool, Brian Holdsworth from Leeds, Robert MacNaughton from Halesowen and Alan Parkinson from Barrow in Furness, who were stationed in the Cameroons alongside me and supplied invaluable photographs of our little adventure in the tropical jungle country.

I say thank you to my other son John and my ex wife Edna for all their encouragement when my spirit was flagging. Special thanks also go to my son Craig for designing my front cover and for setting up a website for my book.

My thanks are also due to Alan Parkinson for his detailed personnel account whilst out on patrol, as described in chapter six.

Finally I thank you the readers, for giving me the confidence to write yet another story.

INTRODUCTION

Dear readers, *Elephant Grass* is the story of personal experiences that I endured in the British Cameroons, West Africa, during my National Service Days. Cameroon was a very poor Third World country and most of the people lived in little mud huts. Many of them were farmers but some were herders of cattle. The terrain on the western border is mountainous from Lake Chad in the north to Mount Cameroon in the south. The North Country is tall grasslands whereas the south is tropical lowlands, but the central region is different again, covered in thick tropical jungle conditions.

I never expected to be writing yet another book; but thanks to you I've got the confidence to do so. My first book, *The Broken Biscuit* was the story of my mother's life how she raised a large family during the Second World War years in the era of clogs and shawls. Its success was far beyond my expectations; I received many letters from all over the country, as well as Spain, America, Australia, and each one asked me to write another story. What gave me the most satisfaction was that I'd brought a little pleasure into other people's lives. I would like to take this opportunity to thank all you kind people for your wonderful inspiring letters.

My second book, *Cracks in the Ceiling*, finished off with me marching off to the Cameroons in West Africa. The reason why I finished my tale at that point was because from then on my life changed completely. I was leaving all the cotton mills, factory chimneys, cobbled streets and poverty of post war Britain behind me. But for the next eight months I was to work alongside even more impoverished people living in little mud huts, struggling every day for a bite to eat. Yet despite terrible poverty these indigent people were friendly, loving and generous to a fault … I'll let you judge for yourself.

John Cowell

DEDICATION

*I dedicate this book to
my two sons,
and all my grandchildren.*

CHAPTER ONE

ARMY DISCIPLINE

Thoughts of my childhood flashed through my mind as I sat on the train heading back to Plymouth in Devon, having just spent a few days on embarkation leave in Burnley, my home town. Despite the abject poverty of my youth, I could only remember the happy times growing up in 14 Albion Street with my three sisters and two brothers. We were poor, but there had always been love in abundance, and I wouldn't have swapped it for anything. Suddenly my life had taken a dramatic turn about, and everything seemed topsy-turvy. During the last year Mum had moved out of our home of twenty years, set amongst the cotton mills and cobbled streets of Trafalgar, into a council house on the Rosehill Estate, I'd been called up into the forces and, saddest of all … my dad had died.

Now at twenty-one years of age, travelling back to camp with the world at my feet, I was on my way to a foreign land with a feeling of eager anticipation, which was tinged with some foreboding. My excitement stemmed from the fact that all my life I'd lived in the most congested part of an extremely busy cotton town, and for the first five years of my working life had toiled underground in the wet and dusty conditions of a coalmine, but now new horizons beckoned me.

Factory chimneys dominated the town's skyline, belching out thick dense smoke from umpteen weaving sheds, covering the cobbled streets and small cluttered houses in grime. The damp atmosphere of the town made it an ideal location for the cotton trade, as the humidity was good for weaving cloth. Most townsfolk lived in back-to-back terraced houses that had been specially built in the 1840's for the mill workers. The squalid conditions had taken their toll; many people suffered from arthritis, bronchitis, emphysema and

11

other crippling diseases, so the prospect of going to a sunny climate thrilled me.

However, my anxiety was paramount because I, along with my mates, was being shipped off to the British Cameroons in West Africa. There had been a recent uprising in the Belgian Congo and the British and French Cameroons were seeking independence. Our mission was to keep the peace during a plebiscite, which was to determine whether the British Cameroons would join Nigeria or the French Cameroons. Terrorist activity was rife on the British and French border, but it was far worse within French territory. I liked the idea of going abroad but I didn't fancy going to a war zone.

"Bloomin' éck," I murmured to myself, "I can well remember all those tales mí grandad used to tell me about the First World War. U-um, the poor soul went away to that bloomín' war full of enthusiasm, but according to what he told me it was horrible!" I felt very deeply for my grandad, as he'd spent four long years living and sleeping in cold wet trenches on the Western Front, seeing many of his mates killed in action and many more dying due to atrocious conditions.

The 'rat a tat tat, rat a tat tat', of the train wheels temporarily interrupted my thoughts, but it wasn't long before my mind started to wander again.

"It might not be as cold in Africa as it was in France for mí grandad, but I still don't fancy going into battle against anyone." A shudder ran down my spine as I imagined hundreds of Zulus charging at me wielding long spears and machetes. At least I wasn't alone in my quandary as I was to find out later.

Fourteen months earlier I had received official papers from the War Office in London, conscripting me into Her Majesty's Forces, to serve two years National Service. Against my will, the powers that be placed me into the Royal Army Medical Corps (RAMC). My title was now Private Cowell, number 23633183. I protested strongly, requesting to be put into another regiment, but to no avail. Nevertheless, it turned out all right. After a few months I settled down and actually enjoyed working as a nursing orderly in the army hospitals.

On enlistment I'd reported to Queen Elizabeth Barracks in Crookham, Hampshire, where, along with more young men, I underwent sixteen weeks of rigorous training. By the end of the

12

rugged course we were all well versed in First Aid and certain nursing duties. It was during this time that I made friends of Jimmy Mitchinson from Wigan, Brian Holdsworth from Leeds, Robert McNaughton, better known as Rob, from Halesowen, Johnny Church from Liverpool and many others. After completing the rigid training I was posted to Seaton Barracks in the Crownhill area of Plymouth, along with some of my new-found friends. It was at my new posting where I met Ernie Christie, a lad from my home town, and he was the fittest soldier on the camp. After a day's slogging he would think nothing of doing a ten mile run just for the fun of it. During the summer months I used to join him, and we spent many hours on Dartmoor trying to break in some of the wild ponies; it was like being out Wild West in a bucking bronco competition.

"C'mon John," he said one Saturday, "let's have a run over to Princetown where the prison is; you never know, we may see some of the prisoners."

"I don't think so Ernie," I replied, "there's a lot of life-timers in there and some are murderers."

"Ah well never mind, it'll still be interesting to see the prison."

"Yeah fair enough then, let's go!" So we set off, and to my surprise we did actually see some prisoners doing menial gardening jobs away from the confines of the jail. We actually talked to one of them and he was only in his early thirties. He informed us that he'd already served ten years and that he was now a trustee with only two more years to serve. I didn't ask him what he was in for, but the thought crossed my mind that twelve years out of his young life was an awful waste.

During the next few months the arduous regime continued; I worked in field hospitals, setting up tents on the bleak expanse of Dartmoor. Besides the fieldwork we did long route marches trekking over grasslands of the moor, which were criss-crossed with muddy tank tracks. The vast area of wasteland was made up of peaty soil covered with heather, bracken and moss. On many an occasion, after footslogging until sunset, we just bivouacked down for the night in the middle of nowhere. One day, after traipsing for hours, we had to make our way through a swamp that looked like the Strait of Gibraltar ... I didn't need rocking to sleep that night.

Other days, dressed in full battle regalia, we spent hours on an army assault course climbing hanging nets, prior to crawling through muddy pipes on our bellies and had to negotiate countless other obstacles. Consequently we were in peak condition and ready to be posted anywhere in the world at short notice. In our case it happened to be the Cameroons. Rumours of the uprising spread quickly throughout the barracks, and within 24 hours the camp was placed on emergency standby. Standing orders notified us that we had to report in batches to the medical centre for inoculations against various tropical diseases. Word spread round the camp that during the First World War, Cameroons became known as 'the Whiteman's grave' because so many men had died due to the many infectious diseases that were prominent in that part of the world. A law had since been passed that any English soldier being shipped out there could, under no circumstances, serve more than nine months. This gave rise to further anxieties.

"Bloomin' 'eck, I'm not looking forward to this." I moaned as we all queued in lines for the dreaded needles.

"No neither am I," whined Rob, "why do we have to have 'em anyway?"

"Because you wouldn't last two minutes in Africa, that's why you bloody dimwit," rapped a corporal who was standing behind us, "especially once you're out in the jungle."

"I take it you've been abroad before?" I asked.

"Yes I have, twice in fact ... but even I have to have a top up because there are loads of diseases over there that we're not immune to."

"How many do we have to have," asked a rather nervous looking soldier, "I can't stand needles ... does it hurt?"

If he was looking for sympathy he didn't get it. "Three," scoffed the corporal, "and yes, it does hurt ... they use the bloody longest needles they can find."

The poor bloke turned as white as a sheet and his distress was enhanced as two other lads teased him.

"I've heard that the vaccine they give you for yellow fever is like treacle and it kills when it's going in!"

"Yeah and it throbs like mad for hours afterwards, and the one for smallpox is worse than that," laughed the other.

14

Others joined in with the ribbing and the poor bloke trembled like an aspen. I was anxious as well and had butterflies in my stomach, but I still felt sorry for the lad. However, fate then took a hand. What happened next reminded of something my dad used to say to me when I was a young lad.

"What goes round our John comes round. Do a bad turn in this life and somewhere along the way it will rebound back onto you."

Well it certainly did in this case. The nervous lad had his injections without any undue reactions, whereas the two blokes, who had been teasing him, flaked out and had to be laid out on a bed. Even the corporal took dizzy and had to sit down on a chair.

All the lads laughed, as the nervous lad went up to him and said, "Are you alright corporal, is there anything I can do for you?"

After the ordeal lots of other lads had slight reactions and had to retire to their bunks.

Colonel Peck, our commanding officer, granted everyone embarkation leave, but gave strict orders for us to report back to camp at short notice. After being issued with railway travel warrants for the homeward and return journey we all eagerly made our way to the railway station. I'd been home on leave a few times before, but this occasion was different; I was aware that I wouldn't see my family again for some time, but the thought kept crossing my mind that I may never see them again. Bearing that in mind I was determined to enjoy every minute of my leave at home with my loved ones. Incidentally, during this particular period, I started a relationship with my future wife on the Saturday night in a large dancehall.

I'd spent just a week at home and thoroughly enjoyed myself when I received the order summoning me back to barracks. So here I was heading for Plymouth, full of mixed feelings as the train wheels thundered over the steel tracks. I landed in Plymouth at seven o'clock that night giving me ample time to catch the last bus to Crown Hill. The camp was bustling with activity and two days later at two o'clock in the morning came the final order … we were on our way.

Despite the early hour, excitement reached fever pitch as the storeman kitted us out with tropical gear. Raised voices resounded through the air as thirty soldiers climbed into the back of three

Bedford trucks that were waiting at the ready to transport us to Southampton Docks. Filled with anticipation the troops broke into song as we passed through the camp gates, heading in convoy to our destination. Not quite knowing what to expect, I once again felt nervous and uneasy.

"Hey what's up John ... are you all right?" asked Brian Holdsworth. "Your face could stop the Town Hall Clock."

"Bloomin' éck Brian ... does it show that much?" I replied feeling a little embarrassed.

"Aye it does ... I thought you'd have been o'er the moon at going abroad."

"I am, I am ... honest! It's just that I've got bloomin' butterflies in my stomach and I can't shake 'em off."

"Yeah so have I, but never mind eh ... we'll feel better once we're on the ship with some ale in our bellies ... just you wait and see."

"Aye I know we will Brian ... thanks a lot. I didn't realise you were feeling the same as me."

"I am that John ... can't you hear my knees knocking?"

"Good lad Bri. Anyroad, are you gonna give us one of your songs ... it'll perk us all up?"

Brian was a big lad weighing over sixteen stone but he had the voice of an angel. He was a gentle giant and his voice, like his nature, was soft, sweet and mellow.

A silence descended over the truck as he began to sing.

"Ma-ma ... I want to tell you that I'll always love you,
Ma-ma, now we're apart I'm always dreaming of you.
I think of the days when I was just a kid,
We were so happy together.
Who cared for me with such tenderness,
No one my darling but you.
Ma--ma, oh how I miss you now that we are apart,
Ma--ma ... so wonderful,
You'll always find a place in my heart,
My Ma-ma ... my own ..."

16

You could literally hear a pin drop as he sang. I looked around at the expressions on the men's faces … men from London, Birmingham, Liverpool, Manchester, Scotland and other places. They were down to earth men, tough as nails … but as Brian sang in his sensitive touching way, tears welled up in their eyes and rolled down their cheeks … and I was no exception. It got me thinking that's there's no one like your mam when you're away from home. I perked up a little when I realised I wasn't the only one feeling jittery, a tingling sensation ran down my spine. As I looked at these men, all unashamed, I realised that they, like me, were also feeling melancholic.

****

CHAPTER TWO

THE DEVONSHIRE

The quayside was chaotic with hundreds of soldiers milling around. Kitbags, ship provisions and baggage which accompanies all armies, were lying alongside great big heaps of everything imaginable. Men were shouting and whistles were blowing. Order, characteristic of army life, seemed to have broken down. All this activity took place in the cover of our ship, the *Devonshire*, which loomed like a leviathan waiting to devour the agitated, ant-like throng scurrying around in its mighty shadow, waiting patiently to create order out of chaos.

As we alighted from the back of the truck, soldiers were darting hither and thither amongst the hustle and bustle trying to organise themselves. Amid the confusion I dropped my kitbag right into the path of a burly sergeant.

"Pick that up on the double soldier!" he bellowed, his handlebar moustache twitching.

"Right sergeant," I replied, not wanting to get on the wrong side of him.

"What regiment are you from?" he barked.

"The medics," I spluttered clutching my kitbag, feeling like Stan Laurel.

"The medics? I might have known ... the Girl Guides have arrived have they!"

The remark raised a few eyebrows amongst my mates, but as he was a sergeant it was ignored. Name calling and barracking was something that the Medical Corps had to put up with. It had been a regular occurrence at Seaton Barracks and many a fight with other regiments had ensued; however, most medics could handle themselves and we had gradually gained the respect of our peers.

18

But that was back in Plymouth … it now appeared that we would have to go through the same rigmarole yet again.

"It looks like we'll have to stick together lads," said Brian addressing all the medics, "at least till we get to know them, and them us."

"You should have told that bloody sergeant to get lost!" snarled Ken Smith, venting his anger at me.

"Oh yeah sure … like you would have done!" I snapped back.

"What do you mean by that remark Cowell?"

"I mean what I say Smithy!"

"Come on lads," put in Jimmy acting as peacemaker, "let's not fall out amongst ourselves. Like big Brian said … we've got to rally together and watch each others backs, you know the score."

"You're right Jimmy," I replied, and turning to the soldier, "I'm willing to let it go if you are Ken … how about it?"

"Aye course I am John, sorry for opening my gob in the first place. Let's shake on it and put it down to nerves."

"Cheers Ken," I said offering my hand.

Whilst waiting to board the gigantic monster, my mates and I put our kitbags on the ground and sat on them.

"Blimey," spluttered Rob taken aback by the immense size of the ship, "how the flamin' 'eck can something like that float … it beats me."

"That's what I was thinking," added Bri, "it's solid steel and must weigh a million tons."

"Come on Bri, what did you expect to carry a battalion of soldiers," quipped Jimmy, "a flamin' rowing boat?"

"Good one Jimmy, you'll make a comedian one of these days."

Our little intermission was interrupted by the same snotty sergeant. "Come on girls get your arses onto that bloody gangplank now … at the double!"

Bri and Ken gritted their teeth and nearly rose to the bait but knew better than to get involved. I was tempted to ask Ken why he hadn't said anything to the sergeant but thought it would be better left alone.

We made our way up the gangplank of the great ship and for moral support our group of thirty medics gathered together on the deck's portside. Our tiny group was dwarfed by six-hundred troops

19

from the King's Own Border Regiment and other attachments like the REME, (Royal Electrical Mechanical Engineers) the Catering Corps, the Signals and the Royal Army Service Corps. We even had some ladies from the Queen Alexandra Royal Army Nursing Corps (QUARANCS).

It soon became evident that Quarancs weren't well liked in army circles because of their supercilious behaviour. Most of them were newly enlisted young women who had just recently qualified as State Registered Nurses in civilian life. The reason for their haughty manner was due mainly to their protective rank. On enrolment into the army they had been endowed with the rank of 2nd lieutenant, whereas a man with the same qualification was only made up to the status of a sergeant. As far as rank was concerned a 2nd lieutenant was three steps higher than a sergeant in the promotion ladder. But the main difference was that a sergeant came under the status of a non-commissioned officer, whereas a 2nd lieutenant was a commissioned officer who had to be saluted. This instant leap to fame appeared to trigger off their conceit. I'd had a run in with them during my training days for not saluting one of them in passing. She immediately took offence, and after dressing me down, put me on a charge.

I got three days' jankers. Jankers was the term given to extra fatigues over and above the normal chores of a working day, plus confinement to camp. I wasn't the only one; the same thing happened to a few of my mates. It didn't take long for soldiers to refer to the high and mighty women as snotty nosed bitches and other well chosen names.

On the *Devonshire* there was one medic to every twenty troops, which was rather daunting, but our fears were soon laid to rest as they turned out to be a friendly bunch and we soon became one big happy family. Then again, under the circumstances, common sense prevailed. We were all being shipped off to a war-torn country and knew only too well that our very lives depended on each other down to the last man … it was reminiscent of the comradeship I experienced whilst working in the coalmines.

Within two hours the last rope dropped from its mooring and the ship started to stir as its massive engines roared into action, edging slowly away from the quayside. The ship was huge and as I stood holding the rail it made me feel small and vulnerable. Looking down I pondered on how many young soldiers had left this dock in the past and never returned. There was no one on the dockside to wave us off, but we all felt it was a memorable occasion as a strange wonderful silence descended onto the deck. The ambience transcended throughout the entire ship rendering all the men passive and mellow.

It put me in mind of a similar situation that had happened to me years earlier when I was a young boy of six. It was announced over the wireless that Germany had surrendered and that the war in Europe, which had lasted six long years, was over. Spontaneously, hordes of neighbours from every household, many in their nightclothes, gathered on the front street to celebrate the joyous occasion. The crowd soon swelled to hundreds as more people flocked from other streets, all making their way to town. I, along with my dad and my brothers and sisters, followed these happy souls. The festivities were unforgettable as flags and bunting festooned the streets, and thousands of happy people danced merrily away to the sound of brass bands, the clashing of dustbin lids and men playing mouth organs. At that young age an indelible impression was stamped firmly onto my impressionable mind. Just like now a huge crowd, which was thronged mainly outside the town hall, spontaneously sank into the same indescribable silence as if synchronised from above.

My thoughts were interrupted as big Brian started to sing,

'Now is the hour for me to say goodbye,
Soon I'll be sailing far across the sea.
While I'm away,
Please remember me!'

After clearing our throats we all joined in, singing in harmony with Brian. It was the strangest of feelings to hear the melodious voices of hundreds of young men all tuned in as in a choir, making the atmosphere sublime. The singing continued as we steamed slowly through the Southampton waters into the Solent where we espied the Isle of Wight in all its glory. It was shrouded in mist, but still looked beautiful. As the ship steered slowly through the cold

21

waters of the English Channel, the first leg of our 3000 mile journey, we all seemed to unite, forming a common bond with each other.

We were soon brought back to reality ... we'd hardly put out to sea before various corporals started yelling out orders for us all to fall into different ranks on the main deck. One of them, Corporal Murphy, took charge of our small group and shepherded us in single file down some steel staircases to a long confined section of the ship, which contained three tier steel bunk beds on either side of a narrow aisle. He then seemed to gloat as he pointed out that this was our sleeping quarters.

"Flamin' 'eck," grunted Jimmy Mitchinson, "this is like being on a submarine!"

It was too – right in the very heart of the ship; portholes were the only form of natural light. On entering I got an instant feeling of claustrophobia, more so than I'd ever experienced whilst working down the coalmine.

"Crikey!" I thought. "I don't fancy sleeping in this chicken coup for the next three weeks ... there's not enough room to swing a cat round."

The bawling corporal interrupted my dilemma, "Right you scruffy lot, as far as some places are concerned this is the Ritz ... make the best of it because this is as good as it gets!"

"You must be joking like," said Mick, a Liverpudlian, "I've got a dog back home that sleeps in better conditions than these."

Not to be outdone the quick witted corporal replied, "Oh have you now? Well let me tell you ... when you've finished your stint in the army you can go back and sleep with your dog, but whilst you're here this is where you'll kip. Anyway, like I said ... it doesn't get any better, and until we reach Africa this is going to be home sweet home. So don't forget to keep the place tidy and that includes making up your bunks every morning."

"Oh aye, and what about you," asked Jimmy, "I suppose you've got a room all to yourself?"

"Ha ha ha!" he laughed. "I can assure you I don't get special treatment because of my stripes ... there's only one bloke who gets a room of his own on a troop ship and that's the captain. If it makes you feel any better, that's my bed over there, the first on the left."

22

After giving us a few more instructions his attitude became much friendlier and he even displayed a funny sense of humour, creating a good atmosphere ... eventually our 'chicken coup' took on a different light.

Corporal Murphy was in his middle thirties and a regular soldier with fifteen years service under his belt. It soon became evident that his nickname was 'Spud Murphy' and also that he was an alcoholic ... his favourite breakfast was two cans of beer. When he stripped off, he sported two tattoos on his chest, nothing complicated ... just the word 'Bitter' under his right nipple and 'Mild' under his left one.

"Right Brian," I said after packing my meagre belongings into a small bedside locker, "I'm going on a walkabout to discover the layout of the ship; how about you?"

"Aye righto, it'll be good to get a breather after being stifled down here."

"I'll come with you as well," said Jimmy, "anything to get out of this rat hole."

When we reached the deck we were well out at sea and England's shoreline was barely visible.

As I stood clutching the rails I shuddered as a fear of the unknown enveloped me. Once again I started to panic and a shiver ran down my spine. "I wonder if I will ever see home again," I mumbled to myself.

"Are you alright John," asked Jimmy, "you seem miles away?"

"Yeah, sorry Jimmy ... I'm just feeling a bit jittery, that's all."

"Tell me about it." he laughed.

Just then we heard lots of happy voices.

"Where's all that laughter coming from?" asked Brian.

"I don't know Bri but let's find out."

To our delight we found lots of lads drinking and smoking in a large concert room, which housed a long bar.

"Yippee, I'm into that," said Brian. "how about you John?"

"Too true Bri lad, like you said when we were on the back o' that Bedford truck ... we'll feel a lot better once we get some ale in our bellies."

As I approached the bar I met up with two mates from my home town who were serving in other regiments. The first was Martin Grogan, which wasn't surprising because I expected to see him on the ship, as I'd had a night out with him whilst home on embarkation leave.

"Hiya Johnny, I've been keeping my eyes peeled looking out for you … I'd an idea I might find you in here."

"Great to see you Martin, the last time we met was down the Nelson Imp wasn't it … I lost you in the crowd once we got inside the ballroom?"

"Aye, it was heaving wasn't it … what a fab night."

"It was that Martin … how did you go on?"

"Superb, I met a lass called Mary Smith and I took her to the pictures the following night."

"Oh aye, go on … tell me more."

"Well I liked her and we had a couple more dates and decided to write to each other whilst I'm abroad in the Cameroons. Anyroad, how did you fare?"

"Well believe it or not Martin, a similar thing happened to me. There was a girl in the dancehall called Edna Simpson, whom I've fancied for ages but never had the courage to ask her for a dance. But anyway that night I thought it'd be stupid not to, 'cos I knew I wouldn't be back in England for a while. Just like you I took her out on the Sunday night and twice after that, and 'Bingo' you've guessed it … we decided to keep in touch whilst I'm in Africa."

"Good lad John, come on … let's drink to it."

"Yeah fair do's, I'll go along with that … are you having a pint?"

"No pints on this ship John, they only have cans."

"Whatever, as long as it's ale I don't mind. Anyroad Martin, this is my mate Brian from Leeds," I said as Brian edged his way to the bar.

"By 'eck Brian you're a big lad … I wouldn't like to get on the wrong side of you. Anyroad, pleased to meet you … any friend of John's is a friend o' mine."

"All I can say to that," Brian laughed, "is you're not very choosy about the company you keep are you? Anyway, what are you drinking, I'll get these."

"Cheers, I'll have a can o' lager."

We were merrily drinking away when things got even better.

"Hiya Johnny," a voice called from behind me, "I never expected to see you on this ship."

On turning I saw it was Neville Atkinson, a friend of mine who'd been in the same class as me at Towneley Technical High School. "All right Nev," I spluttered in disbelief, "how's it going … are you with the King's Own Borders?"

"No, but I'm attached to them … I'm in the Signals. And you, what company are you with?"

"The medics."

"Oh the cushy mob," he laughed.

"So they say Nev, so they say, we'll have to wait and see … ask me again in six months time and I'll tell you then. Anyroad, it can't be any cushier than being in the Signals."

"Yeah you could be right there John … I hope so."

"Are you joining us Nev?" asked Martin who also knew him from back home.

"Yeah why not … in for a penny, in for a pound, as they say."

Our little gathering swelled, and as the merriment continued the conversation turned to the duty-free prices.

"This is great!" laughed one of the infantry lads holding a can of ale in one hand and a canister of cigarettes in the other. "Fifty fags for half a dollar and Senior Service at that."

"Blimey!" said another lad. "That only works out at about ha'penny each."

I couldn't help thinking that my dad would have lapped this up and been in his glory.

"I think I'm going to like being on this boat," put in Martin with a grin on his face.

"Aye, so am I," said big Bri, "cheap fags and cheap booze … great isn't it?"

"I don't know so much Bri," I said, "it seems too good to be true, I can't see it lasting … there's gotta be a snag somewhere."

"Don't put a damper on it John," he laughed, "enjoy it while you can … make hay while the sun shines."

"He may be right," moaned Martin, "I can't see this lasting the duration of the voyage, they're bound to come up with something. Anyway, what about guard duty and fatigues?"

"Don't worry about that," said a regular older soldier, who'd overheard our conversation from the next table, "I've been on a troopship loads o' times afore and it's a life o' Riley. You've got to keep your bunk tidy and do some physical training on the main deck every morning, but that's about it."

"Surely someone's got to do guard duty or kitchen fatigues?" I asked.

"Aye that's true but that's left to the infantry mob. And even they only have to do one stint 'cos don't forget there's six-hundred men to share the task."

"Great!" responded Brian, Neville and me at the same time.

Martin didn't have the same enthusiasm, "Bloomin' 'eck! That means that I might cop for it."

"Aye if you're unlucky," replied the regular soldier. "Anyhow, even if you do you'll only have to do one stint at the most. The rest of the time you can spend sunbathing, playing games, drinking or whatever takes your fancy. Like I said … it's a great life."

"U-um, that'll do me," I giggled inwardly. I was happy but I made a pact to keep myself in good shape by regular daily exercises; it would have been easy to become complacent and fall into the trap of self-indulgence with all the cheap ale and fags about.

My mind went back to when I first joined the army. Out of my meagre allowance of twenty-five shillings I'd allotted seven shillings to my mam back home. In return for this the army made it up and granted her a pension of three pounds ten shillings a week for the duration of my time in Her Majesty's Forces.

The army had a policy whereby they paid out to the nearest five shillings and put the remainder into 'credits'. I didn't mind this, as it was a kind of saving-up scheme, which I could call upon if need be. Nevertheless, it meant that I was only left with a paltry fifteen shillings in my hand from which I had to buy toothpaste, razor blades, soap or whatever. Consequently, I could only afford to go out for a drink on payday and had to scrimp for the rest of the week. After six month's service I got a rise of ten shillings, which eased the burden somewhat. Then after serving twelve months I got a further ten shillings rise; this coincided with being shipped off to Africa, which meant that I got an additional bonus in the guise of an overseas allowance. I was now on nearly four pounds a week ... I felt like Rothschild.

After the night session we all returned to our sleeping quarters only to find that they didn't appear quite so dingy anymore. Whether it was the effects of the beer I don't know, but they now looked all right to me and I was asleep within five minutes of getting into my bunk. Next morning I awoke to the sound of a few lads making their way to the washroom, whilst most of the others were still in bed snoring away.

"Oh boy, this is great!" I thought. "Life on the ocean waves ... I don't think I'm going to miss dear old Blighty after all."

Jimmy Mitchinson, who bunked in the bed above mine, was beginning to stir. "All right John, what time is it?" he asked clutching his forehead.

"Eight o'clock Jimmy ... are you coming for breakfast?"

"U-ugh, forget it! The very mention of food makes me feel awful, I've got the ding-dong of all hangovers."

"Right Jimmy, I'll see you later then." I didn't ask Brian if he was coming because he was sleeping like a baby. I hadn't drunk quite as much as them, and besides, breakfast was one of my favourite meals. Dinner and tea were favourites too ... I loved my grub.

Sure enough at ten o'clock, just like the regular soldier had informed us, we all had to report to the main deck for a session of physical training. After the workout a voice resounded over a loud speaker bringing us to attention, whereby the commanding officer addressed us from the ship's bridge:

"Right gentlemen, you all seem to be enjoying yourselves and that's the way I want it to be for the next two weeks until we reach our destination. But I give you fair warning, don't abuse my hospitality ... I need you all to be in prime condition when we reach the Cameroons. First of all there will be a roll call on deck every morning to make sure no one has fallen overboard. During the voyage, other than physical training and attending educational lectures, you will only have light duties to perform so I want you all to feel relaxed. Mind you, you may have other menial tasks to perform should the need arise. Don't be fooled, I'm not a soft touch and I won't tolerate any indiscipline. You may wear shorts and strip down to the waist for comfort once we reach warmer waters. But take heed! Anyone who gets sunburnt is liable to finish up on a charge of self-abuse. Another thing, I expect you all to comply with army regulations regarding personal hygiene … this includes having a shave every morning. Furthermore, despite the relaxation of duties, remember you are still in the army and under orders from your direct superiors … so behave accordingly. Finally, I would just like to add … enjoy it while it lasts because once we reach the Cameroons you'll wonder what's hit you!" On that note he dismissed everyone.

Loud cheering echoed throughout the ship as the message was received in high spirits.

"I'll tell you what John," said Jimmy, "I'm gonna enjoy this voyage, it's like being on a cruise … all at Her Majesty's expense."

"Yeah me too," chipped in a few lads in unison.

Well that was it, we really did have a good time over the following two weeks, lazing about on deck, swimming in a small pool or anything else that took our fancy … it was great.

****

A funny incident involving Rob and the troop deck sergeant had us all in raptures. This evolved because the non-commissioned officer was the spitting image of Private Doberman from the popular television series 'Sergeant Bilko'. The troop deck sergeant not only looked like his famous counterpart facially and bodily, but he also tended to have similar funny mannerisms. Because of the striking resemblance the troops had bestowed him with the nickname 'Doberman'.

Rob and I were so used to hearing him referred to in this manner that we actually thought that Doberman was his real name. Henceforth, one day Rob dropped a clanger that raised a few laughs and got us out of a spot of bother at the same time.

Deck games and indoor sports such as table tennis were encouraged during the voyage, whilst snooker, darts and cards were played in the concert room. But gambling was strictly forbidden under penalty of reprisal. Still, this pastime did take place, but mainly on the troop decks away from the watchful eyes of our superiors. This particular incident came about whilst we were idling our time away.

Rob came up with a suggestion, "John, I've got some spare cash just burning a hole in my pocket ... let's go and join the lads below deck for a gambling session."

"Yeah, why not ... we may get into trouble but sod it!" So, regardless of the consequences, off we went.

We soon became involved in a session of three-card brag and after twenty minutes I was quite excited, as I was three pounds up. But my enthusiasm came to an abrupt end as one of the lads on lookout raised the alarm.

"Watch out ... there are two officers coming!"

Panicking, we got rid of the cards by stuffing some under the mattresses and others into bedside lockers. Within a moment Captain Gedding and Lieutenant Olsen confronted us.

"What's going on here?" rapped the captain.

Rob was the nearest person to him and started blabbering that we had been discussing what life would be like in the Cameroons.

"Don't give me that," the officer snapped, "I'm not falling for that rubbish!"

"But Sir," stammered Rob, striving to come up with an excuse.

"Never mind trying to bluff your way out of it soldier, I wasn't born yesterday. Anyway, who's your troop sergeant?"

"Troop Sergeant Doberman," replied Bob much to the lads' amusement.

"Troop Sergeant Doberman?" queried the captain, looking rather puzzled. "I've never heard of him." Turning to Lieutenant Olsen he asked, "Do you know this Sergeant Doberman?"

Furrowing his eyebrows the lieutenant answered, "No I don't, I haven't a clue ... he's definitely not an infantryman, maybe he's a medic."

Addressing Rob again the captain asked, "This Sergeant Doberman ... is he a medic then and what's he like?"

By this time my mates were all looking at the ground trying their hardest not to laugh. At first I wondered what they found so amusing and then it suddenly became clear ... especially when Rob started to describe the man.

"Well Sir, he's little and stubby and has a round face with a cheesy grin and he talks with a squeaky voice."

I realised too that the captain had clicked on, as I noticed a smirk at the corner of his mouth.

"O-oh Sergeant Doberman, I know who you mean now," he smiled. Turning again to the other officer he asked, "And you Lieutenant Olsen ... do you know who he means now?"

"I certainly do," he replied, trying to suppress a giggle.

The funniest part was that by now everybody had cottoned on .... except Rob. At least it defused the situation and, instead of putting us all on a charge, the captain let us off with a caution. But before he left he added, "I'll let it go this time lads but don't let me catch any one of you gambling again or so help me I'll throw the book at you!"

"Ha ha ha, that was a good one Rob," all the lads roared at once ... Sergeant Doberman! Where the bloody hell did you dig that up from?"

"Dig it up from, what are you talking about," Rob asked rather bewildered, "is that not his name?"

Well that triggered the lads off again; everyone was in stitches, including me.

"Come on John, what's so funny ... I don't get?"

"Oh come off it Rob," I stuttered in between fits of laughter, "you're not usually so thick. The TV show – Sergeant Bilko and Doberman ... you know what I mean." Then at last the penny dropped. To give him his due though, even he saw the funny side of it.

For days after we all had a good laugh at Rob's expense ... especially when Troop Sergeant Doberman strutted around the deck.

****

It was on the *Devonshire* that I had my first taste of curry. The cooks, all of Chinese origin, specialised in the art of oriental dishes and spicy foods.

"I fancy sampling a curry today John," said Bri, "how about you?"

"Not on your life," was my initial response, "I've heard they can burn a hole right through your stomach."

"Don't be so soft, I've been told they're really tasty. Anyroad, when in Rome do as the Romans do, that's what I think."

"In that case you try it. I'll stick to fish and chips and sod the Romans!"

"I might just do that. Anyroad, how can you knock what you've never tried?"

"Maybe I haven't Bri but I know some lads who have and they were sick afterwards."

"Please yourself John but I'm gonna have some anyway."

True to his word he did try some and surprisingly he loved it; from then on it became his favourite meal. It got me to thinking that perhaps I should try it too… maybe I was missing out. So I did test the exotic dish to discover that it really was tasty. I only had mild ones at first to whet my appetite but quickly acquired a taste for the hotter ones … they certainly got to my taste buds, the spicier the better. From then on I had a curry dish whenever it was on the menu … those oriental cooks certainly had the knack of conjuring up superb dishes.

But cooking wasn't their only specialty as we found out to our benefit. Every evening they would parade about the decks shouting, "D'hobi d'hobi, anyone for d'hobi?"

"What are they on about Bri," I asked as loads of lads joined in a chorus imitating our oriental friends.

"I don't know; let's go and find out."

"D'hobi," said a regular soldier, "that means washing. If you've any dirty clothes that need washing they'll do it for you quite cheap."

It was too. Jimmy, Bri and I mustered up a bundle between us and it only cost two shillings.

"Hey, this is great," said Bri when we got our clothes back, "they're really clean."

For obvious reasons the Chinese were bestowed with the nickname, 'The D'hobi Men'.

****

It was a mild August night when we left Southampton docks and sailed down the English Channel towards the open waters of the Atlantic Ocean; but within a few days the temperature rose steadily. The passage was quite smooth until we reached the choppy waters of the Bay of Biscay, where it became rather bumpy with huge powerful waves driving onto the deck. Despite its size, the *Devonshire* bobbed up and down like a cork in the vast ocean. It wasn't as bad as I expected it to be, but all the same, many of the men were lying on their bunks due to terrible seasickness. Others were being violently sick over the side of the boat. My stomach felt queasy and gurgled a little, but other than that I felt fine. The fact is I actually enjoyed the crossing, as it gave me a feeling of being superhuman. Unlike many other lads, who had had a skinful of ale the previous day, I hadn't touched a drop. I couldn't settle in the sleeping quarters as they stank, with ashen faced bodies lying about on their bunks. So I decided to go up on deck for a breath of fresh air. I stayed well away from the rails for fear of being washed overboard, but clung tightly to palings of central structures. The immense power of nature thrilled me as the wind whipped up gigantic waves and sea spray lashed into my face, making me feel fresh and rejuvenated. An almighty wave hit me so hard I almost lost my grasp. But I was still undeterred ... in fact it made me more determined to ride the mild storm. I imagined I was a crimson pirate as the refreshing feeling invigorated me ... I felt alive and vibrant.

Many lads couldn't eat anything, but I never missed a meal.

"It's time for some grub lads," I laughed as I nudged Jimmy and Bri who were both sprawled out on their bunks.

"Ar-rgh, how you can eat anything is beyond me," moaned big Bri, "I feel like I'm dying."

"Yeah me too," groaned Jimmy, "let us die in peace."

"Please yourself," I joked, "are you sure you don't want me to fetch you a fatty bacon butty or something?"

"Get out of here you bloody sadist before we strangle you," they both screeched at once.

"I'm going ... I'm going."

After crossing the bay the wind settled and the waters calmed down. On sighting the coast of Northern Spain the weather improved daily, and from thereon in the sun shone brightly amidst a clear blue sky, which reflected off the most vivid turquoise sea that I'd ever seen in my life. To my sheer delight a shoal of dolphins started to follow the boat diving in and out of the ocean waves ... the frolicking of these wonderful creatures was a sight to behold. I couldn't help but think of God and the beauty of nature ... the sheer magnificence of it all astounded me, taking me back in awe.

32

"How anyone *cannot* believe in the Almighty when they see such wonders is beyond me," I thought as I felt some sea spray gently splashing my face. I've always counted myself lucky because never in my life have I ever doubted the existence of God or the life hereafter, and at that very moment I felt His presence all around me.

Sailing by the shores of Portugal the ocean appeared even bluer and, against the backdrop of the coastline, it stood out like a beautiful painting. As I strolled around the deck, Martin and Neville were sprawled out soaking up the hot sun.

"This is great John, you can't beat it," laughed Martin, peering over his sunglasses, "what do you think?"

"Well it definitely beats working down the pit," I laughed. "I can't get over the colour of the sea … it's so blue and absolutely stunning."

"Yeah it is isn't it; it's like being in a dream."

"You can say that again," laughed Bri arriving on the scene, "I feel like I'm in Paradise … I've never had it so good."

He was right too. Everything was perfect … and to top it all we had money in our pockets.

"Are you going to join us Bri," chuckled Martin, "this is the life!"

"I sure am," he answered stripping down to his shorts.

"Be careful lads, you know what the CO said about getting sunburnt," I joked.

Just then someone tapped me on the shoulder; when I turned around it was Ted Bennett, another lad from Burnley. I'd met Ted eleven years earlier in a convalescent home in Blackpool where I'd spent two weeks with my older brother Jimmy. It was a home for under privileged children and Mum had arranged it with the school authorities. It was the one and only time I'd ever been on any kind of holiday and I loved it, especially playing in the sand dunes on the seashore. As it happened Ted was there with his younger brother Alan, and as the two boys were in a similar situation to ours, we hit it off right from the start. After our little vacation, as the years passed right into our adulthood, we'd always acknowledged each other whenever out on the social scene.

"Hiya Johnny, long time, no see," Ted greeted me, "I never expected to see you on this boat."

"No, you neither Ted. Which regiment are you with?"

"I'm in the infantry the same as Martin."

After going through the same rigmarole as I had with Neville I had to smile somewhat. "I'll tell you what it is Ted, us Burnley Ites'll be taking the ship over if they don't watch it."

"You could be right there," he laughed. "Anyroad, at this rate those bloomin' terrorists in the Cameroons had better watch out."

At that we all started laughing. By now I had really settled in with no more nerves or anxiety about what lay in store for us, just contentment.

"I believe the entertainment committee is putting on a good show in the hall tonight," said Ted, "is everybody going?"

"Yeah why not." we all agreed, "it'll make a change from boozing."

It turned out to be a great night with all the acts being performed by soldiers. Some lads had previously worked in amateur dramatics in Civvy Street prior to receiving their conscription papers, but most were from ordinary working class backgrounds. One lad stood out from the rest; he was a born comedian with a dynamic sense of humour and had us all in stitches ... we nicknamed him 'Clowney'.

At the end of the show they put on a talent competition, inviting anyone to join in. Brian sang a medley of songs and went down a treat, coming in second to Clowney. He touched the heartstrings of all the soldiers as he sang tender love songs with tears rolling down his cheeks. Despite his big bulky frame, once he started to sing, a silence descended around the room. Just prior to being called up into the army he had got married, and he was terribly lovesick for his new bride. All the lads used to take the Mickey out of him but, no matter, every time a love song came over the radio the tears would appear. Being one of the most sensitive blokes around and also one of the friendliest, he became very popular amongst the troops.

Someone volunteered my services and I sang a couple of songs from the musical, *South Pacific*, which I'd recently seen in Plymouth. In the film, Mitzi Gaynor had dressed up as a sailor and sang *Honey Bun*. I liked the song and sang it whilst Clowney pranced about the floor wearing a hula-hula skirt, waggling his hips. I didn't win any prizes but the lads seemed to enjoy it and so did I.

****

CHAPTER THREE

A SPELL IN THE BRIG

Despite the comradeship and harmony amongst the men the odd fight was inevitable, due mainly to the effects of alcohol and bravado. In most cases the arguments were sorted out by the intervention of other soldiers not wanting things to get out of hand. After the two opponents had cooled down they usually shook hands and the matter was forgotten; otherwise, for further entertainment, it was sorted out in a boxing ring. Even so, on one occasion two really powerfully built chaps got to brawling on the deck, and the fight got so aggressive that the other lads couldn't control it. By the end of the fight, chairs, tables and remnants of broken glasses lay strewed around all over the place. Within minutes the military police arrived on the scene and the two offenders got marched of to the brig.

The next day they appeared before the commanding officer on a charge of disruption, the destruction of property and fighting and he sentenced them both to seven days detention in the cells with loss of pay. To most soldiers the loss of pay was more of a deterrent than the actual imprisonment.

When I heard the outcome of the charge it took my mind back to when I received the identical sentence whilst serving at Seaton Barracks in Plymouth just months earlier for disobeying an order. Just a few days prior to my sentence, Colonel Peck, the commandant, sentenced me to three days' jankers for not polishing my cap badge properly. I didn't question his decision because I was guilty of the trivial offence and felt I could do the jankers stood on my head. In my case I had to report to the orderly sergeant's office at 19-00hours and do two hours working in the officers' mess. This didn't concern me, but what did was the confinement to camp whereby I had to report back to the orderly sergeant at 23-00hours before going to bed.

The first two nights, Monday and Tuesday, didn't bother me, but having to check in on Wednesday did.

Soldiers completing their two years stint in the army always got demobbed on a Thursday, and as Wednesday was payday, a leaving celebration always took place on the same night in the 'Cherry Tree', a pub near the town centre often used to give soldiers a good send off. On this particular Thursday, Colin, a friend of mine, was due to be discharged and I didn't want to miss out on the festivities.

As it happened the orderly sergeant in charge on that Wednesday night was Barry Smith, a lad who had joined the army the same day as I had. He was a qualified pharmacist, which automatically entitled him on enlistment to be made up to the rank of sergeant. When I reported to him at 1900 hours, I mentioned how I felt about my mate's farewell do.

"E-eh, I'll tell you what Barry," I moaned, "I'm really pissed off about not going to Colin's send off party, we've been buddies ever since the first day I arrived here in Plymouth. I don't mind having to wash all the greasy junk, but having to report back here at 23-00hours is a real bind."

"I know how you feel John but there's not a right lot I can do about it. I will say though, they're having a special do in the officer's mess tonight so there'll be a mountainous pile of pots and pans to wash ... if you get through the lot I'm willing to turn a blind eye if you don't report to me tonight. Mind you, if anything goes wrong ... then on your own head be it!"

I didn't need telling twice ... as far as I was concerned, a nod was as good as a wink.

"Great," I said to myself looking at the enormous task in front of me, "just watch me get through this lot." I rolled up my sleeves and worked furiously until I'd cleaned the last spoon, finishing, more or less, on the stroke of nine. Without giving it a second thought I then ran all the way to the Cherry Tree.

Colin was glad to see me but a little surprised, "How have you managed it John, you're supposed to report back to the orderly sergeant at 23-00hours aren't you?"

"Not to worry Colin," I reassured him, "I've sorted it."

"Are you all right John," asked Bri, "what are you doing here?"

After explaining the situation to him we got down to some serious drinking and singing, and by the end of the night we were all three sheets to the wind.

"I hope you'll be OK mate," said Colin as we made our way back to camp, "I'd hate to think you got into trouble on my behalf."

"Don't worry about it Colin, Sergeant Smith said he would turn a blind eye, so I should be all right."

But I couldn't have been more wrong! As we walked through the camp gates I was singled out by the military police.

"What's your name and rank soldier?" rapped a brawny corporal towering over me.

"Cowell, Private Cowell," I answered knowing full well that something was amiss.

"Private Cowell what soldier!"

"Oh, Private Cowell … Corporal."

"Attention," he screeched, "get your arse into the guardroom at the double you slimy little creep … quick march, left right, left right!"

This particular MP was notorious for putting prisoners under his charge through hell. He stood over six feet tall and as he yelled through gritted teeth he looked awesome. He delighted in grinding men into the ground, and for a moment his overbearing presence made me feel intimidated and subdued.

As soon as I entered the guardroom I saw Sergeant Smith sitting at a table looking rather sheepish and by his side sat the regimental sergeant major, who was fuming. I had to stand to attention in front of them both.

"Right Private Cowell, I'm charging you for being absent without leave," rapped the RSM.

"But Sir ….."

"No buts! I made a flying visit to the orderly sergeant's office at 23-00hours and you didn't report there, and it's come to my attention that you left the camp without permission."

I couldn't say much, as I was in a catch 22 situation. It seemed fruitless to protest, because after all, Sergeant Smith had left the decision with me. I couldn't allow myself to bring his name into it; that wouldn't have been the right thing to do … and anyway, I

37

couldn't come up with anything that would have made a difference, so I said nothing.

"Right Private Cowell, you're on a charge and you'll appear in front of Colonel Peck at 09-00hours. If you're one minute late you'll be in even more trouble than you are right now ... understood!"

"Yes Sir."

Turning to the MP he rapped, "Right, take him away; get him out of my sight!"

"Yes Sir," the smarmy bloke replied with a smirk on his face.

As the burly corporal frogmarched me towards the door I glanced at Sergeant Smith from the corner of my eye only to see him sigh with relief.

The following morning I had to go in front of the Commandant yet again, but this time on a much more serious charge than my previous one.

The orderly sergeant gave his version of events, but obviously didn't mention anything about our conversation. I couldn't see any point in divulging it either; the way I saw it I was in trouble whatever I said. After listening to the RSM's statement I knew mine was a lost cause.

Colonel Peck was a fair-minded man and had been very sympathetic with me when my father died, but on this occasion he was angry ... very angry indeed.

After a severe dressing down he sentenced me to seven days incarceration with loss of pay.

The lanky corporal seemed to derive sheer pleasure from the outcome, knowing full well I would be under his power for the next week.

"Pick your feet up you scumbag," he shouted as I strutted across the camp towards the guardroom, "I'll make a soldier out of you if it's the last thing I do!" He stalked over my every movement, striving to insert fear into me with his constant bellowing.

On many occasions I'd seen him frogmarching other prisoners at the double around the camp in the same aggressive manner and each time a shudder had run down my spine. Well this time it was my turn to be on the receiving end of this barbaric creature's abuse.

"Don't let the bastard grind you down John," I thought, "you've had to contend with bullies before."

During my childhood I'd had to put up with many barbed comments in the schoolyard due to the fact that my dad was a rag and bone man and had been to prison twice. Children can be very cruel and I certainly had to learn how to stick up for myself. Well now I was a young man and a strong one at that, so I certainly wasn't going to let this harsh brute dampen my spirit; from that moment I was determined to use his bullyboy tactics to my own advantage so as to turn the frustration back on him. I made it a challenge ... it was either him or me and I certainly didn't intend to succumb easily. The strange thing is I actually enjoyed the next seven days of confinement; but then again I had help from above in the guise of Tommy Wilkins, an inmate ... and what a character he was.

"Now get that uniform off," bellowed the MP, throwing some grey denim pants and a shirt at me, "and put these rags on!"

"This shirt's too big," I complained, "and it's moth-eaten."

"Shut your mouth you little shit," he growled as he opened the cell door, "and get in there with that animal!"

This was my first meeting with my cellmate Tommy, a rough looking character with a stubbly beard. Tommy just put two fingers up to the corporal and grunted like a chimpanzee, baring his teeth.

"Bloomin' 'eck!" I thought as the MP slammed the door shut and turned the key. "Who the hell's this ...what have we got here?"

The only natural light in the cell came from a small window in the steel door and a barred window fixed high into the outer wall close to the ceiling. Other than the cell door we were enclosed within a 13-inch thick wall. The ambience of the cell appeared rather depressing, but Tommy soon changed all that.

He was five feet seven inches tall the same as me with a similar stocky frame, but other than that he was totally different, with a full shaven head like Yul Brynner, and tattoos covered his arms, back and chest. My first impression of Tommy was that he was coarse and unfriendly, but I was wrong. Underneath the bravado lay an affable, warmhearted, generous bloke with a mischievous sense of humour ... we hit it off almost immediately. It soon became apparent that he had a definite rebellious approach towards authority ... especially this corporal.

Tommy didn't beat about the bush, asking "What's your name and what are you in for then?"

"John," I replied and went on to tell him what had happened.

"So you're only in for a week eh … a part-timer?"

"Aye that's right … and you?"

"Just a month," he replied casually.

"Bloody hell, a month!" I spluttered, "that's a long time in'it?"

"Ha ha ha! I could do that in my sleep … the last time I did three months."

"Blimey! What did you do then?"

"I was fighting in the NAAFI Club near the docks and I laid out a couple of sailors. The military police became involved and it took four of 'em to arrest me and bring me in."

"The MP's aren't very fond of you I take it?"

"You can say that again, especially this dickhead of a corporal … I hate him!"

"I know what you mean; he's got a right callous streak hasn't he?"

"He has that, he's notorious all right and he loves the reputation … he's a right sadistic bastard! I've seen many a man break down and cry because of his barbaric ways, but I personally wouldn't give him the satisfaction. Even when he's getting to me I just grin at him and it really goads him … I love it!"

"You know something, similar thoughts went through my head as he was marching me over here stomping his feet."

"I hope you do stand up to him without flinching, it'd be great to have a bit o' backup."

"Yeah so do I; there's one thing for sure, I don't intend to bend to his will."

"We'll see," laughed Tommy, "I've heard many a bloke say that but they always cracked under the brutality of the evil git!"

"Thanks very much Tommy … that's all I need to know."

Tommy didn't mean to be intimidating … it was just his way. "Listen lad, I believe in getting to the point and calling a spade a spade. What's the use in pussyfooting about … he's a right bastard and you might as well know it from the word go."

"Yeah right Tommy, I know what you mean. I've got to admit that he puts the wind up me but I still intend to stick up to him."

"Good for you. Like I said … we'll see. Anyway, it'll be good to watch."

"We will see," I thought to myself, "I'm determined not to let the barbaric thug break my spirit." I didn't either but those seven days tested my will power to the hilt.

"Hang on a minute, that'll be the pig now," said Tommy as a key turned in the cell door, "he's probably coming back for you 'cos he enjoys putting prisoners through their paces on their first day in nick."

"Right you measly excuse for a man," the MP rapped as he glanced into the cell, "out here now at the double and put that on!" he hissed pointing to a large rucksack kitted out with full battle gear.

"Blimey!" I thought as I hitched it to my back, "This must be loaded with stones, it weighs a ton."

The corporal just sniggered knowing full well the rucksack was weighted down.

"Now get your arse outside you friggin' little gobshite and stand to attention till I'm ready for you!"

After standing for an hour, he marched me across to a large playing field, which lay directly facing the guardroom and ordered me to run around its perimeter until he told me to stop. By the time I'd run around it twice I was dripping wet as sweat poured from me. By now it was dinnertime and some of my mates waved encouragingly at me as they made their way to the mess hall.

The slimy MP didn't like the attention I was getting, so took over, "Quick march, quick march you scumbag," he bawled, marching me at the double back to the brig. "That'll do for starters," he retorted, shoving me back into the cell, slamming the steel door shut, "now get back in your rat hole where you belong with that other maggot!"

"How did you get on?" smirked Tommy sprawled out on the bed with his arms behind his head.

"To tell the truth Tommy, I enjoyed it, I got a rush of adrenaline out there ... anyway, it was better than being cooped up in this dingy place." Unbeknown to the corporal, I'd built myself into prime condition since entering the army and I thrived on physical exercise.

"That's good because making prisoners run around that field is his favourite punishment ... it really gets to most blokes."

"Well it won't get to me," I laughed, "I could put up with that all day. Anyroad Tommy, doesn't he make you do it?"

"Does he bloody hell … he's given up on me," he roared laughing.

A few minutes later the cell door opened again and the corporal entered carrying a tray containing two dinners. He handed one to Tommy and then turned to me.

"Get this down your throat and be quick about it!" he snarled. "And don't get yourself settled because I'll be back shortly …there'll be loads o' washing up to do afterwards."

Sure enough, he returned ten minutes later and stood there arrogantly with a self satisfied look on his face, thinking he'd got one over on me. "On your feet you little gobshite … out here now and bring them bloody plates with you!"

"Bloomin' 'eck!" I thought. "He hasn't got a polite word in his vocabulary at all?"

Outside the cell in the main body of the guardroom were six beds where the soldiers on guard duty slept, and a small office to accommodate the MP's. At the back of the room were two toilets and a small kitchen.

"Right you moron, you can wash that lot as well," he snarled pointing to a pile of dinner plates, mugs and cutlery on a wooden table, "and you'd better not break anything!"

After I'd finished he ordered me to carry everything back to the mess hall, which stood at the far end of the camp, and then scrub a large stone floor on my hands and knees with a scrubbing brush.

That night the atmosphere within the cell felt much better because the MP finished at 18-00hours and ordinary soldiers took over until 06-00hours.

Tommy was in a rather giddy mood and wanted to lark about.

"Come on John, let's have a wrestle … I've got a load of excess energy that I want to get rid of."

"No way! It's all right for you, you've been lounging about on your bed all day … I'm knackered. And anyroad, I want to build up some energy to impress our friendly MP tomorrow."

But he wouldn't have it and jumped on me trying to get me into a headlock … nevertheless, I was too slithery and soon we were grappling on the floor, all in good fun. He was very strong but so was I. As we rolled about the floor I could feel his aggressiveness and thanked God I'd kept fit, making us well matched.

"E-eh, I enjoyed that," he gasped after about ten minutes, "it was great!"

After a small respite he began to feel energetic again but this time he started to frolic on his own.

"Watch this John," he laughed, "I'll bet you can't do this." The next minute he started to walk on his hands but after a few yards he tumbled to the floor.

"That's easy," I said, "and I know why you fell over ... you're doing it wrong."

"Oh aye you clever sod ... let's see you do it then."

To his amazement I stood on my hands and walked the length of the room, turned around and walked back again.

"There, what did I tell you Tommy," I smirked feeling cocky.

"Bloody hell! I've always wanted to do it like that ... come on, show me how it's done?"

"Sure why not, you've *almost* got the knack of it now. The trouble is you're not taking your legs far enough forward in front of your head and that's why you lose your balance."

"Go on then, show me!" he blurted excitedly.

"Right, can you see now how far forward my feet are past my head?" I asked after going into a handstand.

"Yeah I can, how come you don't fall over onto your back then?" he asked curiously.

"Well it's something that you've got to get a feel for ... if I'm going to topple over I just adjust my hands forward accordingly. I'll tell you what ... I'll do it again but this time you take notice of what I've been saying."

He watched me enthusiastically as I pranced about the cell before spluttering excitedly, "Right, I'm with you, now get out of the way ... let me have a go."

He struggled at first but with perseverance mastered it and once he got the idea there was no stopping him. It was hilarious to see him prancing around the guardroom on his hands, giggling like a young schoolboy ... I felt I had made a friend for life.

"Watch me John this should get a laugh," he said knocking on the cell door, requesting to go to the toilet. By the time the door opened Tommy was ready and to the amusement of the guardroom

43

soldiers he walked past them on his hands all the way to and from the toilet, leaving them all in stitches.

"That was great," he laughed when he returned to the cell, "they wondered what the bloody hell was going on ... I love it I love it!"

"I've got to give it to you Tommy," I mused, "you've certainly got the hang of it now ... that was a superb performance."

"Yeah it was, wasn't it ... thanks to you John. Anyway, how about another bout of wrestling, I'm feeling energetic."

"Oh come off it Tommy, give us a break after what our friend put me through today."

He just cracked out laughing, "All right, don't have a heart attack ...I'm only kidding!"

"Thank goodness for that!" I thought settling down for a good night's kip.

Next morning after a sparse breakfast the RSM did an inspection accompanied by the smug corporal.

To my surprise the RSM asked me, "Any complaints Private Cowell?"

"No Sir, thank you Sir."

"Bloomin' 'eck Tommy," I said afterwards, "how come he asked me that ... am I in favour or what?"

"No way, it's obligatory."

"How d'you mean ... obligatory?"

"Well it's laid down in the rulebook, he has to ask every prisoner that question ... and you know what a stickler the RSM is for following the rules."

"D'you mean to say he'll ask me that question every morning?"

"That's right, you've got it in one; and not only that ... he has to take any complaint seriously and follow it up."

"U-um, that's handy to know ... very handy indeed."

My newfound knowledge was soon put to the test after I knocked on the cell door requesting some toothpaste, only to be greeted by the corporal.

"Oh you haven't any toothpaste have you not you scruffy little urchin," he snarled sarcastically, "well you'll just have to scrub your teeth with soap won't you!"

"No corporal, I can't do that ... I want some toothpaste please."

"Well you're not bloody well getting any ... understand!"

44

"If you don't get me any then I'm afraid I'll have to report the matter to the RSM in the morning."

"What did you say soldier?" he spat nearly swallowing his tongue.

"I'll have to report ...."

"Shut your mouth you lippy bickering worm and get your arse out here and put that on!" he fumed pointing to the full battledress. "You think you had it hard the other day ... well now I'm really going to put you through your paces."

Once again he had me running around the playing field, and just like before the sweat oozed from every pore of my body. At one point I felt downtrodden but then I thought of Tommy and it spurred me on.

After the fourth time around he stopped me and growled, "Now do you feel like changing your mind?"

There was no chance, as I was now beginning to enjoy it. Other soldiers had yielded under this treatment but most of them were smokers, whereas I'd never touched a cigarette in my life.

"No corporal," I replied defiantly looking him straight in the eyes, "I still want some toothpaste." I knew he was ruffled because I noticed nerves twitching in his face.

"Are you taking the piss you mangy git," he cursed along with a few more choice words.

I said nothing but just stood there staring defiantly back at him. His frustration built up even more and little red blood vessels appeared to erupt in his eyes. His nose snorted as he summoned up more venom from within his big bulky frame. He towered above me and his arms tightened up like steel as he clenched his fist.

I felt like yielding, as his very presence intimidated my whole being, but somehow I managed to hold steadfast. "Stand your ground John lad," I said to myself, "don't let this coward of a man grind you down."

My tactics seemed to be working ... he began to look unsure of himself. For lack of anything better to say he screeched, "Right you little scumbag ... go on, get running until I tell you to stop ... at the double!"

As I ran around the field it came to the notice of some off-duty soldiers and they all started to cheer, encouraging me to plod on in the same way my mates had done previously. There was no need, as once I got my second wind I felt I could go on indefinitely. By now the corporal was panicking somewhat, frightened that I might collapse or something.

"Have you had enough yet you little bastard!" he grunted frothing at the mouth.

"No corporal," I smirked once again looking him right in the eyes, "I'm enjoying this … can I go round again?"

"No you bloody well can't," he yelled, resentment showing in his face, "get yourself over to the guardroom … now!"

When I got into the cell I collapsed on my bed absolutely exhausted.

"Good lad," said Tommy, "well done. I watched you from the cell window by pulling myself up on the bars. That pig of a corporal was bloody fuming … great!"

I didn't get any more aggravation from the corporal that day and the following morning when he did his rounds with the RSM he looked rather passive.

"Right Private Cowell," asked the RSM, "have you any complaints?"

I purposely pondered for a moment, first looking at the corporal, before replying, "No Sir, thank you Sir."

The MP sighed with relief and it clearly showed on his face. After that he relented a bit towards me, he must have thought I was another Tommy … but I still didn't get any toothpaste.

The friendship between Tommy and me made the time spent in the cell more bearable, especially when something happened that I found hilarious.

Tommy was lovesick, having a girlfriend in Plymouth who hadn't visited him since he'd been locked up.

"I've tried writing to her but I'm bloody hopeless with letters, I haven't got a clue where to start," he moaned, "I'm no good at words."

"Just put down what you feel about her," I said as though I was the expert, "girls like to hear nice things you know."

"Hey, hang on a minute you seem to know a bit about it … you write a letter for me!"

46

"Get lost Tommy, I can't do that. Anyroad, she'd know in a crack that it wasn't your handwriting."

"All right then, just say anything that comes into your head and I'll scribble it down."

"Aye, go on then, anything for a bit of peace and quiet," I replied feeling a bit mischievous.

As I spoke out loud he scribbled down on a piece of paper:

My dearest darling Helena, with all my heart I'd like to express my undying love for you but my imagination cannot capture the reality of your being. Your beauty is far beyond words or pen, the elegance of the sun, the stars or anything in the entire universe, and my feeling for you goes far deeper than the deepest ocean. The flowers, the trees, the birds ... everything that is beautiful reminds me of you.

It carried on in this vein.

I was only joking but he literally wrote down everything I'd said, more or less, word for word. I couldn't believe it next morning when he told me he'd posted the letter.

"You haven't written down what I said have you Tommy?"

"Too true I have, it brought tears to my eyes before I sealed it up. If that doesn't do the trick I don't know what will."

"Crikey!" I cringed as I scratched my head, "I hope so Tommy, I really do."

Well, nobody was more surprised than me by what happened next. Helena received the letter and it worked a treat, the following evening she came to visit him and the meeting was all 'lovey dovey, kissy kissy'.

"Success!" I thought, feeling happy for Tommy.

"Thanks mate," he smirked after Helena had left, "that was great, I owe you one ... she's well in love with me again." For the remainder of that night he was as happy as a lark.

The remaining days in the cooler passed quickly and, although I didn't relish being locked up, my time spent there was very memorable but I was glad to be released.

****

Back on the *Devonshire* I was thinking of Tommy when the sound of familiar orders brought me back to reality.

47

"Quick march, on the double, left right, left right you miserable critters!"

I was watching two soldiers being frogmarched around the deck.

"U-um," I thought as I weighed up the two MP's escorting them, "they can't be any more sadistic than that swine of a corporal back in Plymouth."

****

"Hey John," said big Bri one morning, "d'you fancy pairing up with me in a competition of deck bowling?"

"Deck bowling, how can you play bowls on a ship, the flamin' balls will run all o'er the place?"

"They don't play with bowls you silly sod, the game is called quoits and they use hoops made from rope, which you slide along the deck towards a large circular target with a bull's-eye and some outer rings ... like in archery."

"Yeah righto, I'll have a go at that."

Like Bri said, the game involved sliding rope rings along the deck, about the length of a cricket pitch, towards the target. The bull scored 50 and the outer rings scored 30, 20 and 10 respectively. The game must have been invented for Brian and me because we sailed through the early rounds and reached the final without conceding a leg; but we didn't have it all our own way in the final. All previous heats were the best of three legs but in the final it was the best of five. The deck was swarming with supporters, mainly for the two other finalists, who were infantrymen. Nevertheless when Bri and I entered the arena we also got a good reception.

"Come on big Bri, come on John ... show 'em what the medics can do," shouted a few mates in harmony.

Brian and I felt confident and after a few practice shots my bosom buddy said, "Right John, I'm as ready as I'll ever be ... how about you?"

"Yeah Bri, let's go ... we can only do our best."

The other two lads were highly competitive and they took the first leg, winning 21-16. Brian and I dug our heels in and something must have stirred, because after that we ran away with the game winning the next three legs by scores of 21-9, 21-14 and 21-11.

48

Cheers resounded around the deck as we received our trophies and £4 each. The runners up were good sports and congratulated us, saying we played well and were worthy winners.

****

Sailing past the mouth of the Mediterranean we spotted the African coastline but it was just a haze in the far distance. However we later passed a group of islands, which were much closer.

"Land ahoy on the port side!" shouted one of the soldiers.

"Hey look at those islands over there," shouted others excitedly.

"D'you know what they call 'em John?" asked Rob edging near to the rail for a closer look.

"Do I 'eck as like, I haven't a clue Rob ... do you?"

"Yeah, they're the Canaries."

"What, do you mean the Canary Islands?"

"I sure do, you've got it in one."

"Bloomin' 'eck Rob, I wish we were going there instead of the Cameroons."

"Aye, so do I, it'd be great wouldn't it ... I've heard that the young Spanish women are absolutely gorgeous. Cor! The very thought of kipping up with one of them beauties makes me feel like diving in and swimming over there."

"In your dreams," I laughed. "Still, there might be some beauties in the Cameroons."

"Aye, you never know ... I hope you're right John." He giggled like a young schoolboy and then as an afterthought he asked me, "Anyway John, whilst we're on about the Canaries ... why do you think they call them the Canary Islands?"

"Oh, I think that's easy... it's probably because the islands are full of canaries."

"Well you think wrong ... the islands didn't get their names from the birds. In fact it was the other way round ... the birds got their name from the islands."

"What are you talking about ... I don't get it."

"No, I didn't think you would."

"Alright 'know it all' ... are you going to tell me or what?"

"Yeah, fair enough. Well what it is ... 'The Canary Islands' literally translates to 'The Island of Dogs'."

"Dogs! How can it mean an island of dogs?"

49

"Right, I'll tell you a little history of the region. I suppose you've heard about Christopher Columbus?"

"Yeah, he's the fellow who discovered America isn't he?"

"That's right but before that he discovered these islands. When the Spanish began to colonise them they discovered that the islands were full of dogs. There were many different species and some were transported back to Spain to be bred and trained on the king's estate."

"U-um, that's interesting, but it still doesn't explain why they called them the Canary Islands."

"Ah well, that's the clever bit," gloated Rob, "you see it's because the word 'canary' derives from the word 'canine' which means doglike."

"Oh that is clever, I like it … it all fits together now like a jigsaw puzzle. That's a little bit more useless information that I can add to my list of knowledge," I laughed.

"It's all right laughing," said Rob, "it may come in useful some day."

"Yeah, maybe … you never know."

The islands gradually faded into the far distance until they were no more than a blob on the horizon. It certainly was a special time and I felt really good inside. The entire crew took on a happy mood as we gazed across the crystal clear ocean and our joy became even more apparent as once again dolphins joined in the fun, and this time, hundreds of flying fish swam alongside them. Once again I was totally enthralled by the playful antics of the dolphins as they dived and frolicked near the bow of the ship missing it by inches as it ploughed its way steadily through the water. I later learned that the waters surrounding the Canary Islands were ideal breeding grounds for Dolphins due to the depth and various species of plant life.

My geography and nautical terms improved somewhat at this stage of the voyage. In my limited knowledge I already knew that America lay to the west of England and that the sun rose from the east. Everyday I noticed that the sun rose from the left side of the ship over Africa, and every night it set on the right side over the large expanse of the Atlantic Ocean. I was aware that the ship was constantly heading southwards and this got me to thinking.

"U-um, let me see," I pondered, "Japan is the land of the rising sun in the Far East so it must lie over there beyond Africa, and as the sun always sets in the west, America must be over there to the right side of the boat."

"What are you thinking about John?" asked Johnny Walker, a Liverpudlian who'd served five years in the Merchant Navy.

When I told him what I'd concluded he laughed a little. "You're on the right track John, but as you're on a ship why don't you use the proper terms?"

"How d'you mean Johnny?"

"Well for a start, you shouldn't say left or right side of a ship, you should use the terms portside and starboard side."

"And which is which?"

"The portside is always on the left when facing the nose or bow of the ship, whereas the starboard is always on the right."

"That's all very well, but how the hell do I remember which is which?"

"Ah, good question John. I'm not too sure where the name portside comes from, maybe it's because passengers always board ships on that side. However, I'm dead sure about starboard; it literally translates to 'steering side' because centuries ago small boats were formerly steered by a paddle, which hung over the right side of the vessel. So you see if you get mixed up by which is which, just think that you're steering a boat by paddling on the right side and you'll know that's the starboard side ... got it?"

"Yeah, thanks Johnny, that's a really good way of explaining it ... all I have to remember now is which side of the small boats the paddle was on and I've cracked it."

"Go on you daft bugger!"

"Joking aside that was a good tale ... I'll remember it from now on." I did too ... I seemed to be acquiring quite a bit of knowledge from my shipmates on this epic voyage.

Further down the African Coast the ship had to drop anchor in a bay at Dakar the capital of Senegal to take on supplies and top up our water.

Scores of local natives, mostly young boys, sailed out to greet us in small boats and started to dive into the deep water to retrieve pennies that the soldiers were throwing overboard.

51

Others, carrying trinkets and oddments carved from wood, started to barter with the troops to sell their wares. I couldn't make out some of the items from the deck but I noticed a lot of lads negotiating with the natives through the portholes of our sleeping quarters, which were closer to the water. Many of the young boys held up long poles displaying their wares, but kept them just out of reach of the soldiers. Some of the troops, in devilment, pretended they needed a closer look at the object and then tried to snatch it. But the natives were too canny and dangled it just out of arm's reach. Wanting to be in on the action, I rushed down to the lower deck and went into the haggling mode myself.

"You like this?" asked a young boy holding up the sculpture of an elephant beautifully carved out of dark wood. "You give me 3 shillings ... I give you elephant."

"No 3 shillings is too much, I give 2 shillings," I answered going into the same mode of pidgin English.

"No no, 3 shillings is very good price ... elephant take much time to make."

"Yes but I'm not a rich man, I give you 2 shillings ... no more."

"Alright Sir, because you are my friend I do good deal."

"Oh yeah," I laughed, "I'll bet you've got a lot of friends."

"Catch," he said throwing me a piece of string.

"What's this for?" I asked.

"You hold one end, I tie other end to elephant and you pull."

"Oh I see, but what about the 2 shillings ... I throw, you catch?"

"Ha ha ha! You throw in water ... I dive for it."

"But you might lose it."

"I no lose ... you throw, I find." He did too, laughing loudly as he emerged from the deep water clutching the two-shilling piece in his hand.

It was great to watch these young boys as they retrieved the coins effortlessly from the deep-sea water. I used to like diving into the local swimming pool back home to retrieve pennies, but that was nothing compared to this.

They were a friendly bunch all right. After salvaging more coins the young man started to chat with me again and after asking me my name he came out with an expression I'd never heard before.

"You like jig a jig Mr John?"

"Jig a jig ... what is jig a jig?" I asked nonplussed.

"Jig a jig, you know Mr John ... with the ladies," he giggled, grinning from ear to ear like a Cheshire cat.

"Oh jig a jig, I see what you mean ... that's what you call it in this part of the world is it?"

He grinned all the more, "Yes, if you like Mr John I find much ladies for you ... you have plenty good time yes!"

"Sounds good," I replied, "also not so good because we're not allowed to leave the ship till we reach the Cameroons."

"That is very long way ... Cameroons' ladies no good jig a jig like Dakar. I come for you tonight in boat and take you to very nice lady," adding once again, "you have plenty good time, yes?"

"You must be joking, I'd be clapped in irons and they'd throw away the key, but thanks all the same," I laughed.

"Goodbye Mr John," he said as he moved towards another porthole to sell more merchandise.

****

We'd been anchored up about two hours when something extraordinary happened. French planes flew over our ship and dropped hundreds of paratroopers. At first they looked like flies in the sky but as they got closer we could make out definite shapes of parachutes. They all glided systematically inland, presumably landing at their base camp. The display must have been put on for our benefit because it seemed too coincidental that it took place just as we happened to be docking there. I often wondered if our Government had arranged it with the French ... I don't think so but you never know.

It was a nice demonstration and good to watch but another exhibition took place a few moments later, which gained our attention and got us much more interested and excited. A small French passenger ship carrying lots of young women pulled in and dropped anchor on our portside. The decks of the ship were lit up like Blackpool illuminations, and flocks of onlookers showed their interest by cheering and waving at us. This created interest throughout our ship getting lots of the troops excited. We exchanged greetings with them by waving our shirts about and shouting messages. The intensity built up when some mischievous young women started to wave back with articles of underwear from the stern of the boat. They were teasing us knowing full well we couldn't do a thing about it even if we wanted to. All the same we enjoyed the fun of the colourful spectacle, and it gave us all something to laugh and joke about ... it certainly boosted morale. The friendly exchanges took place right up to the moment of our departure when something very special happened.

As our ship's engines roared into action, our lads, once again, started to sing *Now is the Hour*. Just like at Southampton a silence descended upon our ship and it transmitted over to the French boat. At that moment I got an indescribable tingling feeling, which ran from the top of my head to the tip of my toes; and I felt that all the troops and the passengers on the French boat were experiencing the same emotions as I was. It is a memory that I will always cherish and never forget.

That night onboard the lads talked about the paratroopers but the main topic of conversation centred on the French ladies waving their knickers in the air and of course ... 'jig a jig'.

"You like jig a jig, I give you plenty jig a jig," lots of the men kept repeating full of zest.

"I can't wait to get off this ship," said one of the lads. "I'm rampant ... let me get at 'em."

"Aye me too," said another, "jig a jig here I come."

The subject of jig a jig was at the forefront of everybody's mind, including mine, and the matter soon came to the attention of the commanding officer. Next morning he called us all to the deck and we got a lecture from a medical officer.

"Right gentlemen, I know you are all under the impression that the women in the Cameroons are free and easy and this may be the case; but I must make you aware of the dangers. Venereal disease and gonorrhea are rife in this part of the world and if you have sexual intercourse with anyone at all you will be putting yourself at serious risk. The strain of gonorrhea in this part of Africa is very hard to cure as it is resistant to the usual types of drugs we use to combat the disease; and if anyone contracts it there is a serious danger of it turning to syphilis. Another thing, any soldier who becomes infected is liable to be put on a charge."

"That's put me off," I said after the lecture, "I'm going to keep myself to myself till I get back home to dear old Blighty."

"Yeah me too," said Jimmy, "I don't fancy catching a dose ... u-ugh!"

"Go on you soft buggers," said one of the regular soldiers, "don't let a bit o' scaremongering put you off ... they give that same bloody lecture every time a troopship docks, no matter which bloody country it is."

"That may be so, but it's still put me off," I said.

"Well it's not going to put me off, that's for sure," sniggered another lad.

"No me neither," said a few all at once.

We left it at that but later in the dining room Brian spluttered, "U-ugh, this tea tastes bloody awful!"

"Do you know something lads," said Rob, "the bloody swines have gone and put bromide in the teapot."

"Bromide, what's bromide?" asked a rather naive looking lad.

"Bromide is something to stop you feeling randy," laughed Jimmy and Brian, "the CO's trying to put a stop to our antics before we even get started."

"Antics ... is that another name for jig a jig?" joked Rob rolling about in laughter.

"All right, I only asked." said the poor lad, "no need to take the piss." This only made the lads laugh even more.

****

The days passed and eventually the Cameroon coastline appeared on the horizon with a snowcapped mountain in the background.

"Just look at that Rob," I said feeling nostalgic, "it's fantastic in'it?"

"You'll not think so after you've patrolled it a few times John," quipped Rob, "I'm wondering what sort of a place they've brought us to; it looks an ideal habitat for operating terrorists."

"Trust you to think of that. Don't get me going, I haven't had the jitters since leaving Blighty."

Finally we dropped anchor half a mile off shore at Victoria, in the British Cameroons. Like at Dakar, scores of small boats sailed out to greet us; but this time we had more access. It was still forbidden to leave the ship but lots of lads ignored the order and dived into the deep blue seawater.

55

"Bloomin' 'eck Rob," I said, "that water looks cool and inviting doesn't it."

"You're not thinking o' joining 'em are you John, you'll be thrown into the brig quicker than you can blink if you're caught."

"I am that, I'm sure the CO's turning a blind eye 'cos the deck sergeant must have spotted them lads by now."

"On your own head be it John … I know I wouldn't risk it."

I knew he was talking sense but as I looked down at the other lads splashing about in the cool water the temptation was too great. I just couldn't resist it and dived in amongst them.

A few lads climbed aboard some of the natives' boats and exchanged greetings. Laughter soon broke out as the theme of conversation once again focussed on jig a jig.

"You like good jig a jig … I get you plenty?" asked a young boy.

"Young ladies?" asked one of the soldiers.

"Yes very young, very pretty and plenty good jig a jig … I get for you"

"Oh yeah and what's the catch?"

"Catch … what is catch?" asked the young boy? "I no understand."

"What I mean is do we have to pay?"

"Oh yes you pay, but only 5 shillings."

"Five shillings, that's too much!"

"No no, is very cheap, my sister give you plenty good time."

"Your sister!" spluttered the soldier nearly falling out of the boat.

"Yes my sister, she very pretty," replied the young boy puzzled as to why the soldier had reacted in such a manner. To him it seemed as normal as us eating fish and chips back home.

Our conversation was interrupted by Rob shouting down from the deck, "You'd best get yourselves back up here as quick as you can, there's gonna be a deck inspection in twenty minutes."

Along with the others I swam for the ship and started to clamber up the anchor chain. The thick heavy chain ran from the main deck through a two-foot diameter steel funnel piercing the body of the ship.

"Bloody hell!" I thought as I made my way stealthily through the funnel from one huge steel link to another, "I must be crazy doing this ... if the ship moves I'll be crushed like a fly." Was I glad to reach the deck safely. Luckily, we all got away scot free with our little misdemeanor.

After tea we were all summoned to the large hall.

"Come on you scruffy lot!" bellowed the RSM, "this is your last night aboard this ship, playtime's over ... as from tomorrow you're going to find out what army life's really about. Settle down now and take heed, the CO wants to address you ... attention!"

"Right gentlemen, at ease!" ordered the commanding officer, "like the RSM said, life from tomorrow is going to be very different. You've had it nice and easy during our pleasant voyage but things won't be quite so relaxed once we leave the ship ... you're soldiers and I expect you to act like soldiers. Just remember everything that you've been taught in training and work together as a team ... a happy squad makes for a proficient squad. I'd like to point out that once we reach the mainland we will be splitting up to form three camps. The main camp will be set up in Buea, a place about twenty miles up the coast from here where the bulk of you will be stationed. The second camp is in Kumba, fifty miles inland in thick jungle territory, and one hundred and twenty troops will be posted there along with attachments from the Medics, the Signals, the REME and the Service Corps. The third camp is in Bamenda, over two hundred miles from here up in the mountains and I'll be sending many infantrymen there, also with attachments. The whereabouts of each camp has been kept from you for security reasons, but as from now you will find a mandate on the notice board informing each and every one of you of your postings. Finally gentlemen, I'd just like to add ... good luck to you all!"

We were all curious to know which camp we were going to and couldn't wait to look at the orders.

"Bloomin' 'eck!" I moaned. "I'm going to Kumba, right in the thick of the jungle ... is anybody else going there?"

"Not me," said Big Brian, "I'm going to Buea."

"Me too," said Jimmy Mitchinson.

"What about you Nev?"

"No, I'm going up into the mountains to Bamenda," he replied.

"Crikey! Is nobody going to Kumba?" I asked feeling edgy.

"I am," said Rob, joining us.

"Great!" I said. "At least I'll know somebody then ... anyroad, what about Ted?"

Ted's going to Bamenda with me," answered Neville.

It didn't turn out as bad as I feared because seven other medics from our squad were also going to Kumba. Martin Grogan was going to the same posting as me, albeit he was in the infantry. I felt rather sad about Jimmy and Big Bri going to Buea ... they were a good mates and I knew I'd miss them.

"Ah well, at least that's sorted," said Bri, "we may as well meet up tonight in the bar for a last night piss up.... what do you say?"

"Yeah, fair enough," everybody agreed.

"I'm gonna laze around and soak up the sun," said Big Bri, "it may be the last chance we get."

I lazed around with him for a short while, but then spent the rest of the day playing deck quoits with Jimmy. Later that evening, before joining the lads, I walked about the deck, taking in the beauty of the night. A beautiful red sky contrasted with the clear waters against the backdrop of a tree-covered coastline with mountains beyond. Many natives were still bartering with some soldiers, whilst others fished and lazed about in boats nearer to the shore. The silhouette of the small boats added to the beauty and peacefulness that abounded all around. Everything appeared so alluring, tranquil and untroubled.

"It's funny," I thought, "everything about this place seems to be at one with nature and yet we're out here to sort out an uprising."

I then said a little prayer:

"Please God, keep close to me and my friends in this Third World country and protect us from harm. May I always see the world as I see it at this moment. And finally, please keep watch over all my family back home. Thank You God, amen!"

Big Bri interrupted my little invocation, "John, are you coming or what?"

"Yeah all right, I'll be with you in a minute."

"What's up John, you seem to be miles away?"

"Sorry Bri, I was just reminiscing and admiring the sunset, just look at it ... it's absolutely stunning."

"Maybe it is but we've got twelve months to admire it whilst we're stuck out here in this Godforsaken country. Come on let's go for a drink with the other lads to celebrate our last night together for a while."

"Godforsaken," I thought, "how can he say that with all this beauty around?" Nonetheless, I did agree that this was a night to celebrate. "You're right mate, I'm coming."

I'd had the time of my life on this voyage and didn't want to leave the decks of the *Devonshire*. But realising that all good things come to an end, and that this would be the last time we would all be together, I picked up speed and followed Brian to where the lads were having a sing along and a drinking session. The overall mood was melancholic, as for many of us it was the parting of the ways. It was sad because we'd grown towards each other like a family, and didn't know if we'd ever see each other again. Also it was the end of our summer vacation ... we now had to face the dangers of what our time in Africa had in store for us and the uncertainty of what lay ahead.

****

CHAPTER FOUR

THE BRITISH CAMEROONS
- KUMBA

"Come on you lazy lot," shouted Spud Murphy, "time to get up, the holiday's over ... we've got some **real** soldiering to do now!"

Butterflies built up in my stomach again as the truth started to dawn on me. The fact that we were going to a war torn state had been suppressed during the pleasant voyage, but at this moment stark reality stared me straight in the face. My fear intensified as news filtered through that a soldier from the Royal Engineers in an advance party had been killed. Rumours had it that his truck had run off the road into a deep basin ... I never did find out for sure what really happened but, it occurred to me that in this kind of situation, it was inevitable that more of us would be killed. Once again I imagined hundreds of Zulus charging at us wielding machetes.

"Stop it John, get a grip of yourself!" I mumbled as I emptied the contents of the bedside locker and stuffed them into my kitbag. I left the confined sleeping quarters with a tinge of sadness, which struck me as strange, taking into account the way I felt when I first set eyes on the place.

"Come on John," said Brian, "we'd best make our way up to the main deck."

"Yeah righto Bri, just give me a minute."

Before I followed the others I knelt down and said my final prayer before leaving the ship:

"Please God protect me and my comrades during our mission in the Cameroons and keep us safe from harm. I don't want to do any wrong to my fellow man even though he be my enemy, so please be with us at all times and grant us the wisdom to do the right thing under difficult circumstances, should the need arise."

"Say one for me John," said a couple of men tapping me on the shoulder as they passed.

"I have done lads, don't worry about it," I replied rising from my knees.

The deck was a beehive of activity as corporals and sergeants issued orders.

Then the CO's voice came over the loud speaker:

"Attention everybody! All soldiers going to Kumba and Bamenda must assemble in the entertainment hall until further notice. All those going to Buea, remain on deck and prepare yourself for disembarkation ... we leave within the hour."

Before they marched off I bade goodbye to my friends, especially Big Brian and Jimmy.

The lads going to Bamenda vacated the ship next and finally at 14-00hours came our turn. After making our way down steps at the side of the ship we boarded landing boats, which carried us towards the shore. The jungle came right up to the shoreline and the dock was just on old broken down jetty. How nobody got hurt climbing from the boat up an old rickety ladder onto the rotting pier is beyond belief, we found it very difficult trying to negotiate broken timbers whilst carrying full battle gear. To make matters worse the structure was covered in slimy moss, making it very slippery. Anyone overbalancing would have crashed into rocky waters fifteen feet below and could have been maimed.

Several three-ton Bedford trucks were parked ready to take us to Kumba.

The other medics accompanying Rob and me were Maurice Sutcliffe, Mark Radiven, Peter Jenkins, Bill Hupboard, Rodney Marsh and Spud Murphy, and we were attached to 'B' Company.

"Fifty miles to go, we should get there in about an hour," said Bill.

"What time is it now?" asked Rob.

"Five o'clock," replied Pete, "so according to Bill's reckoning we should reach camp about six o'clock."

That's what we thought, but we hadn't taken into account the state of the road ... and it was the monsoon season. It wasn't a road at all ... more a dirt trail, and following heavy rainfalls it was more like a muddy tank track. Halfway into the journey one of the rear trucks got bogged down and it was all hands to the pumps. Unfortunately it was going dark and the only light given off was from fireflies.

It was nine o'clock before we reached Kumba, sludged up to the eyeballs. The campsite was in a jungle clearing and the climate was hot, sticky and clammy. Two soldiers, both with rifles over their shoulders, patrolled the gate within yards of the guardroom whilst another stood to attention at the foot of a long flagpole, which was flying the Union Jack. A corporal marched from the guardroom to greet us but wouldn't allow us to enter the camp until he'd thoroughly examined our papers, scrutinising every document. Weeks previously an advance party of Royal Engineers had built some Australian bush huts, which housed between thirty and forty men; however, the medic's hut was much smaller with only eight beds. The huts, all open planned, were constructed of corrugated tin sheets on a concrete base. We were all looking forward to a wash and brush up after our arduous journey but no such luck; maybe the high ranking officers had warm running water at their disposal, but for us privates there was no chance.

"If you want a wash there's a large water tank at the other side of camp near the latrines where you can fill a bucket," said one of the engineers.

"What, d'you mean we've to wash in cold water?" I asked.

"That's right," laughed a sergeant, "until we get this camp up and running that's the best thing on offer."

"Bloody hell, I'm caked in mud … how the flamin' 'eck am I supposed to get this lot off?" asked Bill.

"Like I said, you'll have to ………"

"I know, don't remind me … I'll have to wash in cold water."

"Yes," said the sergeant, "and don't forget there'll be an inspection parade in the morning so you'll have to turn out presentable."

"Inspection parade? You must be joking!" said Bill.

"It's no joke, you know the rules … this is what you've been trained for."

Just then, much to our delight, we heard the bugler playing, *'Come to the cookhouse door boys'.*

"Great!" I thought. "Time for something to eat … I'm starving."

On our way over we had to jump from duckboard to duckboard to avoid sinking in the deep mud, but even so some of the slime squelched through each individual batten. The canteen was constructed in a similar way to the other huts but was much larger, and built onto the end was the divisional headquarters, housing the commanding officer and other high-ranking officers. The dining area served a double purpose, as in between mealtimes it became the NAAFI Club where the written orders were listed daily. After feeding our faces, my mate Pete and I browsed through them hoping we wouldn't be on guard duty. To my delight I wasn't, but I did have another task to perform.

"Look at this Pete," I said, "I'm on Paludrine duty in the morning."

"How do you mean ... Paludrine duty?"

"Well according to this, I've got to walk alongside the RSM in the morning during inspection parade to make sure every soldier takes a Paludrine tablet to prevent the spread of malaria."

"Hey that's a cushy number in'it, I hope I get to do it."

"Don't worry you will," said a rather effeminate voice from behind us.

On turning around it was a sergeant in his mid thirties, sporting a medic's cap badge.

"Hello boys," he said with an alluring smile, pleased to meet you; I'm the sergeant in charge of the medics."

"Oh right Sarge," I stammered, standing to attention, "I'm John Cowell and this is Pete Jenkins."

"No need for that, you can stand at ease ... I won't bite," he said in a camp manner. He weighed us up and down for a moment before saying, "Anyway, I'll see you both tomorrow morning in the hospital directly after inspection parade ... goodnight, sleep tight the pair of you."

"Blimey!" stuttered Pete. "Where the bloody hell did they dig her up from ... it looks like we've got a matron in charge of us?"

I tried to play the situation down because my dad always told me, "If you can't say anything nice about a person our John then it's best to say nothing at all."

"Don't be like that Pete," I said, "at least she means well and seems to be thoughtful and caring."

"She means well does she John? Oo-ohh, you could be right there."

I couldn't believe what I'd just said but I certainly hadn't said it with malice or forethought. ... it just came out naturally after hearing Pete refer to him in that manner. This was only the start; I'd set a precedent of a pattern to come. After that we made our way to the ablutions where loads of blokes were stood stark naked washing their muddy clothes before swilling themselves down. The engineers had already constructed some shower units made up of bamboo partitions but they were not yet up and running. Alongside them was a line of similar tiny huts which housed the toilets but they weren't what you could call the Ritz. A long deep ditch, which was chemically treated to ward off smells and control the spread of disease, ran underneath each compartment. Wooded arm supports were attached to the side walls to help one to squat down. But we couldn't complain because this was heaven in comparison to what the Royal Engineers had to put up with when they first arrived. It must have been terrible for them having to live in tents and make do whilst they constructed the camp in constant torrential downpours. All credit goes to them. All my mates and I took our hats off to those marvellous guys; they'd done a superb job under extremely difficult conditions and we really appreciated it. They'd worked arduously alongside the RASC, not only to construct the camp, but to make sure we had a steady water supply. All the drinking and service water was from a water tank that had been delivered by the RASC in an Austin K water tanker.

"B-rr, I don't fancy this," I spluttered as I stripped off to have a wash.

"Neither do I," moaned Pete, "but here goes."

The water was freezing yet refreshing as the mud rolled from our bodies down the makeshift drainage holes.

"By 'eck I feel better now," I said as I put on some fresh clothes, "I only hope my bed's comfy." That was wishful thinking.

When we returned to our hut it was dimly lit by a Tilly lamp and the atmosphere was stifling. This part of Africa was renowned for having the most humid climate in the world and it certainly lived up to its reputation. The slightest effort caused me to sweat profusely and I couldn't get any respite from the clamminess. The place was rife with mosquitoes, and to make matters worse the loud whistling of crickets seemed to pierce the eardrums. I wasn't the only one affected by the high pitched monotonous tone, which soon became apparent.

"How the bloody hell are we supposed to sleep with all that racket going on?" moaned Rodney.

"Stuff some cotton wool in your ears," said Spud Murphy, "that's what I do."

"I've already done that and it hasn't made a scrap o' difference."

"Does anybody know how to tuck these mosquito nets in?" asked Maurice, who was very fastidious and always went to bed early, "It's rather awkward from inside the net."

"O-ooh ... rather awkward is it? laughed Spud Murphy as he mimicked Maurice's posh accent. "You'll have to struggle like everybody else. Anyway, make sure you check in between the sheets for tarantulas, they're as big as your fist."

"Oh no, not spiders ... I hate 'em!" he blurted jumping back out of bed in panic.

I understood how he felt, a shudder ran down my spine at the very thought of a big hairy creature crawling about in my bed. I'd always had a fear of spiders, even little ones back home, but the very thought of a tarantula made me cringe. When I was a young boy I used to go every week to the Saturday matinee and loved to watch my hero, Tarzan. He starred in weekly episodes which always finished with him in a perilous situation, leaving me in suspense until the following week. But on one occasion it frightened the life out of me. The chapter ended where Tarzan entered a dark cave and got ensnared in a giant spider's web and the hideous creature was moving ever nearer to suck his blood. Consequently, I never slept a wink that night and had nightmares for the rest of the week. It frightened me so much that I didn't go to the pictures the following week. But I was still intrigued as to what happened and asked my friends. They just laughed and called me a cry baby.

Whilst sailing over here on the *Devonshire* I'd discussed my phobia with Maurice and he'd enlightened me that he also dreaded the furry things. We'd confided in each other and so I understood perfectly how he felt on this occasion, but all the same, I couldn't help but laugh at his funny antics.

His reflexive impulse to undo his mosquito net and whip back the sheets had us all in stitches. All the same he made sure to meticulously make up his bed properly and he smoothed the sheets out with his hands, feeling for any bumps or lumps before climbing back into it.

Rob laughed at Maurice's hilarious capers, "You'll have to get used to things like that, there are loads o' snakes, scorpions and other vile creatures in this neck o' the woods ... or should I say jungle."

The ribbing continued until we heard the bugler playing the *Last Post*. However, because of the humidity nobody could sleep and the conversation got around to our new sergeant.

"Has everybody met her now?" Pete asked.

"I haven't," replied Mark.

"Oh you're in for a treat ... she's a real good looker," said Rob.

"What ... is she a woman then?"

"No is she hell as like, but she certainly acts like one."

"You're having me on ... he can't be all that bad."

"Let's put it this way, if you're ever in the showers make sure it's a cold one," joked Spud Murphy as he downed a can of beer, "and whatever you do, don't drop your soap or else Flossie will have you ... ha ha ha!"

Once again I sprang to his defence but no matter how I tried in my mind I kept referring to him as 'her'.

"Leave it be John," laughed Pete, "just go with the flow," adding, "I wonder if Sergeant Flossie will come and tuck us in before we go to sleep? Goodnight everybody ... sleep tight."

"Ah well," I thought before finally nodding off, "at least they're a friendly bunch, that'll make my stay out here in Africa a lot better."

****

I woke up the next morning to the sound of torrential rain splashing onto the tin roof with water pouring in everywhere and flooding the concrete floor.

"Bloody hell!" I thought as I put my boots on. "How the flamin' 'eck am I supposed to keep these clean for inspection parade ... by the time I've nipped across to the canteen through all that slush they'll be as muddy as ever."

When we were stationed at Plymouth we were all under the direct command of Colonel Peck, but here at Kumba the commanding officer was an infantryman. All medics were still under the indirect command of Colonel Peck but he was stationed at Buea. Our immediate officer here at Kumba was Lieutenant Whittaker, a medical officer.

Luckily the RSM on parade was in a good mood and gave us some leeway, "Right you scruffy lot, I'm going to be lenient with you as far as your boots are concerned due to the muddy conditions, but that doesn't mean to say you can get away with not shaving. As from now I'm going to work your butts off for as long as it takes to get this camp up and running and shipshape." Turning his attention to me he barked, "Right medic, now give every single one of these pathetic critters a Paludrine tablet and make damn sure they swallow it ... understand!"

"Yes Sir ... understood Sir."

The heavy rain continued and by the time I got to the hospital at the far side of the camp I was drenched. But I counted myself lucky to be working in the confines of the hospital.

"Blooming' 'eck," I said to Pete, "I wouldn't like to be an infantryman, working out in that deluge ... at least we're under cover."

"No neither would I, they'll be like drowned rats before long."

"Right everyone, can I have your attention please!" shouted the sergeant.

"Here we go," said Pete, "Flossie's calling."

Hence, 'Flossie' was to stick for the duration of our time in the Cameroons. But the nickname wasn't derogatory ... it just came natural to refer to him that way. Even if a high ranking officer enquired about him the answer would be, "Oh she's in the sergeant's mess" "I don't know where she is" or something similar. But they couldn't put us on a charge for insubordination because they used to answer something like, "Oh is she?" Out of respect, we never addressed him personally in that manner but always with the title of sergeant. He was however aware of his nickname and, far from being offended by it, he seemed to preen himself even more and would proudly trip about the hospital wards with a new swing in his walk. It appeared as though he had gone all lah-di-dah on us.

Anxious to assert his authority the sergeant called us to attention.

67

"Right everybody, listen carefully whilst I go over your duties. I'm Sergeant Burtonshaw and I bear total responsibility for the smooth running of this field hospital. Corporal Murphy will be my second in command and I trust I will have the support of you all whilst working alongside us. Between the remaining seven of you, you'll not only have to cover all nursing aspects of this hospital, which involves keeping the ward covered 24 hours a day, 7 days a week, but you'll also be on standby in readiness to go out on patrol. For every twenty infantrymen sent out to police the jungle, a medic will be attached to them. We've no patients at present but once we have, one of you will have to work night duty. I'll work out a rota so that everyone does his fair share."

"Blimey," said Pete nudging me, "we're going to have to work our balls off!"

During your working hours" the sergeant continued, "some local natives, employed by the army solely in an auxiliary capacity, will assist you. They have been briefed to carry out your orders, but remember this ... they are ultimately my responsibility. I will work alongside you on the day shift, but during unsociable hours you will have to contact me at the sergeant's mess. You will also work hand in glove with the medical officer, Doctor Whittaker, who will run a clinic every morning. I'd like to think that we're going to be one big happy family. Remember ... a happy team makes a proficient team." He paused a little before adding, "Are there any questions?"

"Yes Sarge," said Rodney, "which one of us will have to go out on patrol first?"

"Good question Private Marsh," replied the sergeant trying to remember everyone's name. "Well that'll fall onto anyone who's not on duty at the time, and don't forget you may be called upon in the middle of the night."

"The middle of the night Sarge," I asked, "that begs the question ... do we have to do guard duty?'"

"I thought someone might ask that question Private Cowell. Well you'll be pleased to know that the answer is no ... not whilst you're on hospital duty."

"Great!" I said along with the others.

"What did you mean when you said that the natives have only been employed in an auxiliary capacity?" asked Rob.

"Well Private MacNaughton that means they're here just to assist you but they're not allowed to do any nursing duties. Any more questions?"

"Yes Sarge," I put in, "what are we gonna do today without any patients?"

"Don't fret yourself about that soldier, I'll find plenty to keep you busy."

"Keep your gob shut John!" said Bill prodding me in the back.

"What was that Private Hupboard," the sergeant asked, "am I missing something?"

"No, sorry Sarge, I was just saying to John that it'll give us a chance to familiarise ourselves with the layout of the hospital."

"Good," the sergeant smiled, "I'm glad to see you're taking an interest."

"You wormed yourself out of that one Bill you crafty sod," I whispered.

The entrance to the hospital had a narrow passageway leading off to a doctor's surgery, a treatment room and ultimately a ward with ten beds. This is where the sergeant introduced us to our local assistants, Dominic, Nelson, Mathias, George, Alphonso and Kinton, and what a friendly happy bunch they were.

This was our first chance to talk to the local inhabitants, and I welcomed the opportunity. From the word go they were so polite and easy to get on with. All six made it clear that they welcomed our presence in their country because of the many years they'd been oppressed under Nigerian rule.

The morning passed quickly and before we knew it the bugler was calling us to dinner. Rob had to stay behind whilst the remainder of us trudged across to the canteen. It was during this brief respite that I met Pius Tashi, a young boy in his early teens. He greeted me after dinner as I entered our hut.

"Hello, who are you then?" I asked.

"I Pius Tashi," he smiled, "I like to work for you ... I work very hard."

"Nice to meet you Pius, I'm John but I'm sorry, all the workers from your village are employed by the army."

"No, you no understand Mr John, I no want to work in hospital I want to work here in hut."

"Hang on a minute! How do you mean, you'd like to work in the hut?"

"Everyday I wash clothes, I make beds, I clean boots and keep hut tidy."

This got me interested. "All right young fellow, it sounds good to me, but now for the million dollar question … who pays you and how much?"

"Everybody in hut pay Mr John but only 3 shillings each, every Friday. I work for you six days a week."

"That seems fair enough to me," I replied, "but I can't promise you anything until I've had a word with my hut mates." At that remark I noticed a frown on the lad's face. "Don't be alarmed," I assured him, "they'll be back shortly and I'm sure it will be all right." Within a couple of minutes they had all returned and I explained the situation to them.

"I'm not paying 3 shillings a week outa my pay," moaned Rodney, "the laundry will do my washing for nothing."

"Trust you to come up with that one you bloody skinflint!" said Bill.

"I think it's good value for money," I said, "it's worth that just for cleaning our boots."

"Yeah so do I," said Pete, "let's have a vote on it."

Apart from Rodney the vote was unanimous in the young boy's favour and he made his feelings very clear, especially to me.

"Thank you Mr John, you very good man, I want you be my friend."

"Whoa, slow down Pius, let's wait and see how you get on before you think I'm your friend … if we fire you next week you won't like me very much then will you?"

"Fire me Mr John?" he asked anxiously. "I no like fire … you no burn me."

"Ha ha ha!" we all laughed spontaneously.

In his confusion Pius wasn't amused but when we pointed out to him what we meant he started laughing too.

Over the next few months our hut boy proved invaluable, he was worth his weight in gold and deserved every penny we gave him and more besides. The monsoon seemed to last forever but no matter how muddy our boots were at the end of the day, they were sparkling clean the following morning. Because of the constant humidity everyone was prone to irritating skin rashes caused by prickly heat, especially between the groins, which meant having to change our underpants twice daily. This infection became known as a D'hobi rash.

Consequently, everyday a line full of white underpants could be seen blowing on a line outside our hut. Lots of infantry soldiers became infected with the fungal type rash but not one medic suffered from the complaint.

"Now aren't you glad we employed Pius Tashi?" Rob teased Rodney. "You'd have had the screaming habdabs by now but for that boy ... the laundry's a dead loss and they put too much bloody starch in the water anyway."

Everybody on the camp, including sergeants and officers, took a leaf out of our book, employing a hut boy to do their chores ... it proved invaluable.

****

For the first few days we never had a minute to spare. Even in our off duty time we had to get stuck in with infantrymen, helping to make the hospital more accessible, chopping down trees, laying concrete paths or anything else necessary. We were hampered by the constant heavy downpours, which turned the mud into slush as we trudged through the camp. In the meantime we worked alongside the doctor as he ran the morning surgery and carried out his orders in the treatment room.

The commonest ailment amongst the soldiers was fungal rash, which we treated with Talcum powder and Whitfield cream, advising each soldier on the importance of personal hygiene; in extreme cases the doctor prescribed antibiotics. It wasn't a serious condition but caused a lot of ribbing amongst the troops.

If any lad contracted it the other soldiers would say things like, "U-ugh, get away from me ... I don't want to catch the dreaded Dengi fever." - "Hey look at that fungi in between your groins ... you could bloody well grow mushrooms in it" – "It looks like he's been bit with crabs!"

Then came the complaints of the 'bad boys' suffering from the consequences of enjoying themselves with the local ladies. Many men were going berserk and couldn't stop scratching, as they suffered constant itching caused by pubic lice. As soon as they dropped their pants the tiny varmints could easily be seen scurrying amongst the pubic hairs.

The infestation was an extremely irritating condition and prevalent throughout the camp, driving men frantic with the constant itching. The main treatment for ridding them of the minute critters was to completely shave the pubic and scrotal area until they were like babies again. Thankfully this remedy worked within a couple of days ... much to their relief.

"I'm sorry Joe," I said as I examined one soldier, "there's only one cure for this."

"What's that?" he asked anxiously.

"Well, I'm afraid we're gonna have to cut 'em off."

"What, not my balls ... please don't say my balls!"

I paused for a moment but couldn't keep up the pretence, thinking I'd taken the joke a bit too far, "No Joe you silly sod ... your hairs, your pubic hairs."

"O-ooph, thank goodness for that ... you had me scared there for a minute!"

"Well you will put things where you're not supposed to," I laughed.

"Aye I know, but it's the last time believe me."

"Yeah," I sniggered, "that's what they all say ... you'll be back."

The next complaint in line and far more serious was gonorrhea ... once again caused by sleeping around with the ladies. Each man infected had to go through the same rigmarole as before but this time the treatment was more severe.

"Drop your pants and let's have a look." I said as each man in turn entered red-faced. The most obvious sign was pus, oozing from the urethra. In the early stages the medical officer directed a course of Penicillin injections into the backside, twice daily for a week. This usually worked but if not the doctor then prescribed Streptomycin injections which, during my personal experience in Africa, always worked.

Prior to coming to Kumba the only injection I'd ever given was into an orange so I was a bit nervous at my first real life attempt. I'd been taught way back in training school to always insert the needle

72

into the upper outer quarter of the buttocks so as to avoid damaging the sciatic nerve that runs off the spine and down either leg.

The injection went well ... I never felt a thing and the patient didn't complain. After that I never suffered from nerves again and I gave dozens every week. I had to smile to myself one day when one of the native workers approached me rather sheepishly.

"What's up Kinton, you look worried?"

"It very bad Mr John," he uttered with his head down ... I very sad."

"Well, what is it? I asked curiously.

"It be ... I .... I u-um."

"Come on Kinton spit it out ... it can't be all that bad."

It is jig a jig Mr John ... I have jig a jig with lady and now I think I die."

"I nearly started laughing but I could tell by his face that he was deadly serious. "Oh I know what it is," I smiled trying to make light of it, "you've got a poorly winkle haven't you?"

"How you know Mr John?"

"Never mind how I know ... just drop your pants and let me have a look." Sure enough, just like the soldiers he had the giveaway telltale signs. I knew that I couldn't treat him officially but, what the hell, I was his only hope of him getting treatment.

"Right Kinton," I reassured him, "it's not all that serious and I can help you but you must keep this our little secret ... I'll get thrown in jail if the doctor finds out ... understood."

"I understand Mr John, I no tell anyone ... you good man."

"You'll not think so when I give you an injection," I laughed, now drop your pants again!"

After the shot he was all smiles and sang my praises, "That no bad ... it no hurt," he giggled.

"I wouldn't laugh yet because you'll need plenty more before you've done."

"That alright ... I come here everyday till better."

There's just one more thing Kinton," I said as he was about to leave."

"What that Mr John?"

"Be a good lad," I joked, "no more jig a jig with the ladies eh."

"Ha ha ha!" he laughed now much happier.

During the first fortnight we had to deal with cuts, bruises, insect bites, sunburn, boils and other minor ailments, but then we had a crisis on our hands as soldiers came down with symptoms of malaria. Before the end of the third week, five of the hospital beds were taken up. To top it all, two medics were sent out on patrol along with the infantry, leaving just six of us to cover the ward and other duties. Three of the patients had typical malaria symptoms accompanied by diarrhoea, nausea and vomiting. I did my first bed bath on a semi comatosed patient with the aid of Dominic. Remembering my training I talked the auxiliary through the procedure, stressing the importance of treating the patient's pressure areas.

"It's very important that we turn him every two hours to prevent the skin breaking down and becoming infected. If I'm busy at the time Dominic, don't forget to remind me," I stressed as I turned the patient onto his left side. The strict routine was especially important in the tropical climate, as under the humid conditions the healing process took much longer.

"I no forget Mr John," Dominic said conscientiously.

He didn't either, and it was just as well because two hours later I was busy elsewhere attending to another patient. I was really grateful and complimented him on his efficiency. After we turned the soldier onto his right side I did a four-hourly observation check.

"Blimey," I thought, "he's got a rip roaring temperature and he's sweating like a pig!"

"Is something wrong Mr John?" asked Dominic rather concerned.

"Yes there is Dominic, this soldier is poorly and needs sponging down … can you please bring me a bowl of cold water and a sponge."

"Yes Mr John, I go right away Mr John … I go.......!"

"Whoa, just slow down a bit Dominic," I reassured him, "no need for alarm … he'll be all right."

"Thank you Mr John, thank you … I go fetch now."

That's what these natives were like, obliging, courteous and friendly, and always willing to please … their humility really impressed me.

Things turned out well and within days my patient improved, and was feeling much better. It was a valuable learning experience for me and a good opportunity to build up good relations with the auxiliaries ... not that I needed to, they were superb.

My colleagues and I were only nursing orderlies but the arduous training we had undertaken held us in good stead as we carried out many and varied duties. Besides giving injections we had to treat deep wounds, becoming experts in the art of suturing. Bandaging, checking temperatures, pulses, respiration and blood pressures were all part and parcel of a day's work. It soon became apparent however that we had to deal with a very common complaint. Soldiers were constantly returning from patrols with deep lacerations ... especially to their arms. Some of the wounds were really nasty and needed several stitches. It seemed incredible that the injuries were actually caused whilst ploughing their way through tall grass in the jungle. This grass stood well over six feet high and was known to the locals as *'Elephant Grass'*.

The QUARANCs were fully qualified State Registered Nurses but we never saw them in Kumba as they were all stationed at the main campsite in Buea.

Along with my workmates, I was glad about this because the officer status bestowed upon them had gone straight to their heads making them unbearable to work under. It always struck me as unfair that any woman, upon entering the army as a qualified State Registered Nurse, was automatically promoted to the rank of 2nd lieutenant whereas a man with the same qualifications was only promoted to sergeant. To me it was unfair on two counts:

Firstly, a 2nd lieutenant enjoyed the privileges of a commissioned officer, who one had to salute, but a sergeant's status was that of a non commissioned officer.

Secondly, the way I saw it, an officer's pay was substantially higher than that of a sergeant.

It became the topic of conversation in our tent.

"I don't think it's fair," said Bill. "Why those bitches get preferential treatment over men is beyond me ... I like women but I haven't come across a decent QUARANC yet ... the pompous bitches!"

"I know what you mean Bill," I said, "they're really toffee nosed cows aren't they?"

"They are that … the way they pranced about on the *Devonshire* like prima donnas got right up my nose, I could gladly strangle the lot of 'em. It might be hot and clammy stuck out here in the middle of the jungle but we should all count ourselves lucky that we're not stationed at Buea. Word has it that them bitches are strutting about like bantam cocks giving orders left, right and centre, having the medics running about like blue arse flies."

I couldn't suppress a chuckle.

"What's the joke John … let us all in on it?" said Pete.

"Well what it is Pete, I can just imagine Big Bri working under them bitches, he'll hate being ordered around. He doesn't like hard work at the best of times so he won't like taking orders from women … especially them sort."

"Rather them than us eh?" he laughed. "Sergeant Flossie doesn't seem so bad now does she?" Bethinking himself he asked, "Anyway she's got the same qualifications as them fancy pieces so how come she's not a 2nd lieutenant?"

"Because she … sorry I mean he, is a man," I said becoming tongue-tied. "Anyway, have you not been listening to what we've been saying?"

"I know she, he or whoever, is a man," said Pete, "but that still doesn't answer the question does it?"

At this point Maurice intervened, "If you want to know the reason, it's a protective rank to stop men fronting up to women."

"How do you know that?" I asked.

"Because I've read about it in some army manual. Anyway what difference does it make how I know it, I just do."

"A protective rank?" put in Pete. "They don't need protecting, I wouldn't touch 'em with a bloody barge pole … no way."

"No neither would I" laughed Spud Murphy, "I've been around QUARANCs for a while now and I've never come across a good one yet."

For the grand finale we all agreed that we were better off than our mates at Buea and that Sergeant Flossie wasn't so bad after all.

****

During my free time I liked going to the market about a mile from camp where haggling was common practice ... I soon learnt never to give the asking price. I could have bought two wooden elephants for what I paid for the one on the ship when we were docked at Dakar ... still, I put it down to experience. All the traders tried to sell me their wares, insisting that theirs were the best. Many stalls displayed wooden hand carvings of animals, warriors holding spears, clocks and many other items. I was intrigued by the intricate details of each piece which must, with infinite patience, have taken many hours to make ... the craftsmanship was certainly first class. I'd have loved to buy many items but knew it was pointless, as I wouldn't have been able to get them home.

There were many food stalls, including freshly baked bread and an assortment of tropical fruit. The meat was definitely fresh, as farmers herded cattle to market and slaughtered them to order, slitting the animal's throats in the market place, letting the blood flow into the dirt. It was not a nice scene to witness, but to the natives it was a typical everyday occurrence. The carcasses were then cut up and displayed on the meat stalls with millions of flies buzzing around, whilst the stallholder was often fast asleep. It was only a small village, yet many large Mammi wagons used to roar through it over a potholed road at an alarming rate.

The market was on the fringe of the village with about forty stalls set up by the side of a fast flowing river. The river flowed right through the border separating the British colonies from the French Cameroons. A large stone bridge spanned the water giving access to French territory but to us soldiers it was strictly out of bounds. Every time I looked across towards the French side it fascinated me. I don't know why because it looked exactly the same over there as it did on our side; maybe it was because of the unknown or simply that it was out of bounds ... who knows? I did actually cross over the bridge every Sunday morning to attend the Catholic service, but I, along with other church goers, was driven there in a Bedford 3ton truck. The church was usually packed to capacity and the locals always gave us a rapturous reception; in fact, they reserved a line of seats for us on the front row. I couldn't understand the sermon totally, as the priest spoke in French; I did however get the gist of the Gospel and I could follow the flow of the Mass because, as a child,

I'd been brought up listening to it spoken in Latin. The ringing of bells, prior to and during the offertory, were just the same as back home. I enjoyed mixing with the locals after Mass but, generally, as soon as the service was over, my mates and I were immediately driven back to camp. Lots of missionary nuns always attended the ceremony and on the forthcoming New Year's Day I was to buy a Sunday missal and get every one of the spiritual ladies and a couple of priests to autograph it for me.

Kumba itself was only a small village with mud huts strewn mainly alongside the one and only gritty road with other huts scattered here and there in thick undergrowth. As I walked back towards camp I counted three bars, two small stores and an old brick building, which housed the post office and the Bank of Kumba. The bars, also set back from the road surrounded by banana trees, were the favourite haunts of the troops. I used to frequent them, but always found it rather daunting as I made my way home at night along the dark dirt track, especially if it was a moonless night. It was also creepy because I had to pass the local prison, which was about half a mile from the camp and sometimes I thought I heard a prisoner screaming. It's happen as well that there was only one road to camp because otherwise I'm sure some of us lads would have got lost after having a few drinks.

****

Maurice was definitely the most fastidious lad I'd ever come across. His bed space and belongings were always immaculate, earning him the reputation of 'Fuss Pot'. I used to say my prayers before I went to sleep but, so as to avoid ridicule from my hut mates, I would often say them quietly underneath the bedclothes. Not Maurice, it didn't matter who was there, he would unashamedly kneel down by the side of his bed and recite his offering before retiring. He didn't drink or smoke and always went to bed before nine o'clock. Next morning he would be up like a lark and ready to go before anyone else. He wasn't one for fooling around, but on saying that he was a likeable bloke and a very conscientious worker, precise in everything he did.

One night whilst he was taking a shower four of us were playing cards on one of the beds and we decided to have a joke at his expense. Lizards were forever darting in and out of the hut

78

scavenging for food and they were massive. Pete had recently captured one and had it in a cage under his bed. It was a beautiful creature, green and blue in colour intermingled with black spots, and from head to tail measured about ten inches. It put me in mind of a small prehistoric mammal as its forked tongue slithered in and out of its mouth like a snake.

"How about putting this in Maurice's bed before he comes back?" said Pete. "It'll be a good laugh."

"Good idea," I agreed, "come on then, we'll have to be quick though … he should be back any minute."

"Right," said Bill, carefully pulling part of the mosquito net out and fumbling with the bedclothes, "put it in between the sheets now."

"Make sure you put everything back neat and tidy," said Spud Murphy wanting to get in on the act, "or he'll smell a rat, you know how faddy he is."

We finished just in the nick of time and then sat back around the bed playing cards.

"D'you want to join in Maurice?" I asked, wanting to distract him as he entered the hut wearing a towel around his waist.

"No thanks, I appreciate the offer but I want to go to bed, I'm bushed."

We carried on, acting as normally as we could with one eye on the cards and one eye on Maurice's bed. First of all he got down on his knees and said his prayers and then, still in the kneeling position, carefully pulled out just enough mosquito net to allow himself to crawl under it and into his bed. Once inside the net he drew back the top sheet and carefully edged himself underneath the bedclothes.

"Will one of you tuck my mosquito net in please?" he asked.

"Yeah righto, I'll do it for you Maurice," I said struggling to keep my face straight, "just give me a minute."

"Thanks John, you're a good lad. I'll do the same for you sometime," he yawned, making me feel guilty.

After doing my little deed I quietly retreated to play cards with the lads again. Nothing happened for a while, which got us to thinking the lizard had escaped. But then all hell let loose.

Maurice just grunted at first and then he let out a piercing scream and couldn't get out of bed fast enough. He threw the blankets back and in his frustration pulled down the mosquito net, ripping it.

"You set of bastards!" he roared along with a few more obscenities. We all rolled about laughing; it was hilarious to see him struggling under the collapsed mosquito net. Maurice wasn't amused and he tore a strip off us bawling loudly, "Don't think you're gonna get away with this you scruffy mingy gits; I'll get my own back on you if it's the last thing I do!"

He did as well and I was his first victim. He went about it very cleverly, catching me off guard about two months later just before Christmas when I'd forgotten all about the incident. I was sitting on my bed and he came over to me with a carton of fifty cigarettes in his hand ... or so I thought.

"Could you give me a bit of advice John," he asked in his usual polite manner, "I'm not quite sure what to do?"

"Aye course I will Maurice, what is it?"

"D'you think my dad'll like these for a Christmas present John?" he asked handing me the carton.

"He should do Maurice if he's a smoker ... I can't see why not."

"Yeah, but these are not English cigarettes, I bought 'em on the market and they're brown coloured. Will you just have a look at 'em for me?"

I never suspected a thing. The lid was tight and on squeezing it, it came off with a jolt. To my horror, eight long furry legs suddenly dangled over the side of the canister followed by an enormous black hairy body.

"A-ar-rrgh!" I screeched, temporarily frozen to the spot as a monstrous tarantula dropped onto my lap. "Get the bloody horrible thing away from me!" I then moved quicker than I'd ever moved in my life and cringed as I saw the horrible black monster scurrying across the floor.

"Ha ha ha!" roared Maurice. "Got you ... serves you bloody well right!"

He'd done his homework all right ... his memory of my phobia for spiders, especially big ones like that one, served him well.

He got his own back on the others too ... Pete got a snake in his bed whereas Bill and Spud Murphy got a bed full of ants.

80

We all decided it was best to leave Maurice to his quiet unassuming ways in future.

****

One day, whilst working with Kinton, he asked me if I liked swimming.

"Yes Kinton," I enthused, "why's that?"

"I know very good place Mr John ... you like very much."

"You don't mean the river do you Kinton?"

"No, not river ... it is a big ... u-um, how you say lagon?"

"A lagoon," I queried, "do you mean a large expanse of water like a lake?"

"Yes, very big Mr John ... lagoon."

"And whereabouts is this lagoon then?"

"No very far ... same as market but other way."

"Righto," I said becoming interested, "when can you take me?"

"I no work Thursday ... if you like I come for you."

"Great, I'm working the afternoon shift then ... what time can you get here?"

"I see you at ten o'clock Mr John, you have plenty good time."

"Hey you're not trying to fix me up with a woman are you Kinton?"

He looked a little confused answering, "I no understand Mr John ... we go swimming."

"Right," I laughed, "don't take any notice of me, I'm only joking. Anyway, I'll see you at ten o'clock and while we're at it you can drop the Mr John bit."

"Yes all right, I no let you down ... thank you very much Mr John."

Sure enough, at ten o'clock, Kinton was there on the dot. On leaving the camp gates we turned right, heading in the opposite direction to the market. He took a little detour from the road and after walking for about twenty-five minutes through dense jungle we came to a breach, which gave way to a magnificent sight. There in front of me amidst the forest was a large lake surrounded by idyllic hills blooming with a myriad of beautiful flowers set amongst green vegetation. It reminded me of a film I'd seen years previously, *The Blue Lagoon*, starring Jean Simmons. It turned out to be a crater lake of an extinct volcano.

81

"What about that!" I stuttered in disbelief as the cooling water looked like Shangri-La, "I'm having some of that Kinton ... come on, let's go!"

The setting was perfect, it even had a wooden jetty set out onto the lake with a diving board and fifty yards from the shore was a floating platform anchored by a length of mooring rope. It turned out that some European business people had built it for their own personal use but had recently left. I couldn't wait. I immediately stripped off and dived off the jetty and swam across to the floating platform.

"Come on Kinton," I laughed, "this is great!" He didn't need any encouraging and for the next two hours we had a fantastic time.

The hideaway became my favourite spot and over the coming months I wiled away many an hour there in my free time.

On one occasion I was relaxing on the floating platform listening to the sound of the birds when I heard some young boys shouting for help. One of the youngsters had dived from the diving board and was in obvious difficulty, splashing desperately in the deep water. I immediately dived in and swam to the boy, taking hold of his arms and dragging him to the safety of the shore. After putting my First Aid expertise to full use, clearing the boy's throat I could see that he was all right ... he coughed and spluttered a little but other than that I knew he would be fine. I stayed around for another hour to keep an eye on him but there was no need to really, as within twenty minutes he, along with the other boys, was playing and getting up to mischief.

As I made my way back to camp I was happy with the outcome and felt very good inside. I thought that was the end of the matter but two days later I had visitors. A local couple came to the hut to see me and brought me a bottle of wine. I didn't feel a reward was necessary but the poor kind people insisted, saying they would be most hurt if I refused. I was once again taken aback by their simple humility and even more so when they came out with something that will stay with me until the day I die.

"Mr John, you save life of our son - now he is your son too, you responsible for him all the days of his life ... not his body but his spirit."

I was touched by the gesture and their kind sincerity and promised to keep the boy in my prayers ... after all I was now his Godfather.

At the time I didn't tell anyone about the incident ... it was to be my special secret and my own private legacy and this instilled me with confidence making me feel happy inside; many a time thereafter, if I was ever feeling low I drew strength from it. To this day I often think of that little boy and wonder whatever became of him.

****

Despite the hard work and unsociable hours I genuinely enjoyed my work in the hospital and the camaraderie, especially now that the monsoon season was ending giving way to bright sunshine. However, there was one aspect of army life that I didn't like at all ... going out on patrol. I'll never forget the first time, as I got roused out of bed at 01-00hours. After being shepherded into the back of a truck I, along with twenty infantrymen, a corporal, a sergeant, an officer and a local native tracker, were driven over the bridge and dropped deep into the French Cameroons. I tagged along behind the courageous soldiers like a spare part as they trudged through swamps and pushed their way through thick jungle vegetation. As I pushed aside branches thickly laden with large leaves I was terrified of coming into contact with a snake or brushing up against a tarantula.

Every infantryman was encumbered with a full battle pack on his back and carried an SLR (self loading rifle), which was deadly accurate up to 2000 yards. But the officers and NCOs each carried a Sterling machine gun, which was more effective in close combat; it could fire twenty rounds of ammunition all at once, or one at a time in quick succession ... but was only deadly up to about 50 yards. And here I was carrying the First Aid pack. In a way I was glad that I didn't carry a gun because, put to the test, I felt I couldn't shoot anyone.

"Never mind," I thought, "if we get attacked I'll just have to strangle 'em with my bare hands."

Joking aside I was scared and very wary of being shot by a sniper or being ambushed. Walking in single file at the back of the soldiers through thick undergrowth was frightening, as it occurred to me that in all the films I'd seen about jungle warfare, it was always the man at the back, who got his throat slit first. Actually, none of the soldiers liked being the back man or the *Tail end Charlie* as they used to call it. Not having any option I marched behind the twenty-three soldiers and the tracker over rugged terrain as they hacked their way through thick bush country, and then waded across a river. Being my first time out in the jungle my nerves were on edge and my imagination ran riot, as I picked up every little sound which seemed to be magnified a hundred fold. Fireflies flickered and danced to the piercing music of crickets and croaking frogs. I was used to this sound from back at Kumba, but I nearly jumped out of my skin when a load of monkeys started screeching high up in the trees. It's just as well that I didn't have a gun because I may have let off a few rounds. We'd only been marching a few hours and I already had a crick in my neck caused by constantly peering over my shoulder. To put it mildly I was scared to death, imagining that I'd never see another day. I wondered what I was doing there ... I just didn't seem to fit in at all, I felt useless. But by the end of this patrol I changed my mind.

After traipsing till daylight the officer called us to a halt so he could check his compass and reconnoitre the area.

One cocky lad, who like me happened to be out on his first patrol, approached me and asked wryly, "How are you going to defend yourself medic if we get attacked?"

"I'll have to hit 'em with my handbag," I joked for want of something better to say.

"Bloody good reply medic," laughed Bob Clayton, a regular soldier, who was as strong as an ox and had loads of combat experience, "I like it." He then turned to the cynical bloke and actually blasted him on my behalf, "You've a lot to learn you bloody sprog so keep your bloody stupid remarks to yourself! When you've done as many patrols as I have you'll know that one man you need to have around in the jungle is a medic."

The bloke didn't take too kindly to being rebuffed and, by the way he glared at me, I got the message that the advice had fallen onto deaf ears.

"Not to worry, there are worse troubles at sea." I thought. I then smiled to myself, "maybe I'm not so useless after all."

My train of thought was broken as the officer issued further orders, "Right men, playtime's over let's get going!"

We marched for ages passing solitary mud huts way out in the middle of nowhere.

"It amazes me," I commented, "how anyone can possibly survive in this wilderness, miles from anywhere."

"They probably live off bananas," laughed Bob, "there's loads of banana trees everywhere." It was then that we came across a small patch of land that had been ploughed. "There you are medic he said, it looks like they've got their own tiny allotment."

"What are those tall things growing in the crop," I asked naively, "they look like pineapples?"

"They **are** pineapples you silly sod," laughed the corporal, "are you thick or what!"

"But I thought that pineapples grew on trees like apples, I didn't know they grew in the ground."

"Well you know now you daft bugger!"

Up until that point I'd always assumed that they grew on palm trees, as their trunks look like large pineapples. "Ah well," I thought, "something else to store in my memory box."

Every now and again we came across large columns of ants on the march that appeared from the undergrowth and disappeared some hundred yards further along the track into thick jungle foliage. The columns were about five inches wide and made up mainly of workers, but soldier ants patrolled their flanks keeping them in position. There must have been millions of them, but they didn't bother us if we kept out of their way. During a short break some soldiers started to lark about and they put some lit cigarette ends right smack in the middle of a cluster just to see what would happen. Immediately the workers scattered in confusion but within seconds a number of soldier ants threw themselves onto the burning remnants and smothered the flame. Other soldier ants immediately removed the carcasses and the stubs whilst others reorganised the column. Within minutes they were back on the march as though nothing had happened.

"You silly bastards!" roared the sergeant, "What have I told you about messing about with them critters. We'll have to move on now or else they could be swarming all over us; and believe you me, if you get bit with one of them soldier ants you'll know about it; it's a lot worse than a bee sting."

85

I don't know whether they would have attacked us or not, but at the time it did seem the best thing to trek on.

As we pushed on my throat became parched but I only dared to take a sip to wet my lips as my water bottle was already well down. I could gladly have drunk it all there and then but the veterans had stressed time and time again the importance of conserving water. That small sip tasted like nectar and I was tempted to take a big gulp but knew better of it; it did however test my willpower to the hilt. Eventually at noon we had to stop, as the sun was now directly above us and it felt as though we were in an oven. Despite sitting in the shade of the thick foliage and the green canopy above I couldn't get any respite from the unrelenting heat.

"Bloomin' 'eck," I moaned as sweat oozed from every pore of my body, "I'm bloody well baking!"

"You're not the only one medic," rapped the same bloke who'd ribbed me before. "Anyway, what are you moaning about you flea bag ... you're supposed to be the one looking after us!"

I was too knackered to get into a dispute and just replied flippantly, "Yeah alright, keep your hat on ... oops sorry, I mean your hair!"

"Too bloody true I'll keep my hat on, I don't need you to tell me that," he sneered not catching on to what I meant.

At that a few lads started laughing and defused the situation.

I could understand the lad being ratty because I felt that way myself. I was clapped out, dehydrated, clammy and the humidity was unbearable. To make matters worse, as I tried to wipe the sweat of my brow I noticed some bloody fat leeches, feeding merrily away on my arms. It was my first encounter with these vile critters and they repulsed me. What bothered me most was the fact that I'd never felt a thing when they'd attached themselves to me.

"U-ugh!" I thought. "How many more of these filthy creatures can be attacking me?"

It soon became apparent that other soldiers had unwelcome guests as well, as they vented their complaints at me.

"Quick medic, give me something to get rid of these varmints!" they screeched.

"Just burn' 'em with the lit end of a cigarette you bunch of sissies," laughed Bob, "they'll soon drop off."

"That's alright but how the hell do we keep 'em off?" yelled one lad.

"I don't know about leeches," I said, "but I've got loads of insect repellent in my bag ... maybe that'll work."

"Gimme some," yelled a few at once, "owt's worth a try."

The officer posted some men on guard and advised the rest of us to get our heads down to catch up on some sleep.

"He must be joking," I thought, "with all these creepy crawlies about. That's what I thought but within five minutes I was in 'Noddy Land' along with the others. I was just about to dive into an icy cool swimming pool when my dream came to an abrupt end.

"Come on you scruffy lot, bedtime's over," ordered the sergeant, "we've a lot of marching to do."

After trekking for hours through the sweltering jungle we came across an almost dried up river bed with batches of stagnant pools scattered here and there. Much to our despair the meres were infested with midgies and mosquitoes. We badly needed to rest but had to crash on regardless because these flies were more irritating than the leeches. We ploughed our way through some elephant grass but the plague seemed to follow us; it was only when we began to climb a steep incline that the swarm died down and left us in peace. Only when we were well clear of the minute pests did the officer order a halt. The leeches and the other creepy crawlies were bad enough to cope with but then we encountered another disgusting critter.

"Ar-rg-gh," screeched one of the soldiers as we were sat down taking a breather, "what the bloody hell's this on my arm!" It was a tick. It was the first time I'd come across one and it made me cringe. I'd been told about them back in training school but my knowledge was limited. I did know though that if I didn't remove it the soldier could be in trouble. The vile creature, about the size of a cherry stone, had buried itself beneath the skin. It had already burrowed its way an inch up his arm and left a snail like trail of slimy eggs.

"I'm sorry mate," I said, "I can't just burn it off with a cigarette like we do with leeches; I'm going to have to cut it out."

"I don't care," he panicked, "just get rid of the horrible blood sucking mite."

I rummaged through my medical bag and pulled out a packet of Gillette razor blades. "One of these will do," I thought, "at least they'll be clean." I then tried to put the lad at ease, "Right mate, first I'm going to have to make a tiny slit at one side of the tick and then try to scoop it out with a penknife. I'm sorry but I can't numb it for you 'cos I haven't got any anaesthetic on me."

"Oh flamin' emma, is it going to hurt!"

"Well yeah, but I'll be as gentle as I can."

"All right then; just get on with it!"

I'd never dealt with a tick before but I was aware that they had crablike legs and that it was vital that I didn't leave any remnants inside; otherwise he could get blood poisoning. After dousing the arm with iodine I nervously made a slash at one side of the parasite and then attempted to dig it out with the knife.

"Ouch," he moaned, "be quick!

I prodded about as carefully as I could until I felt as though I was underneath its body and then gently eased it out.

"Is that it, medic, have you got it?"

"Not quite, there's still a couple of legs stuck in there and some eggs; just bear with me for a while longer," I assured him as I picked out one of the scrawny limbs with a pair of tweezers. Surprisingly, both legs came out smoothly just leaving me to flush out the eggs and other crap. "That's it," I said feeling pleased with myself, "it's all done and dusted; all you need now is a plaster to keep the wound clean."

"Thank goodness for that," he sighed, "I can't stand the little parasites."

Not long after that little episode the officer called us to task and, once again, we were on our way.

We climbed steadily for a while finally arriving at a ridge just as the sun was setting. We were all weary and dishevelled but thankfully the officer called a halt, whilst he did another reconnaissance of the surrounding area. After thoroughly reviewing the situation he issued further orders.

"Right men," he murmured softly, "this is the place I've been looking for. About five hundred yards along this track the ridge overlooks a hamlet of about twenty huts and according to intelligence they're harbouring some terrorists. I want you all to bivouac down here now for the night because we're going to swoop down on them just before dawn tomorrow. Now you've all been drilled constantly for this type of operation so you know the score …. no talking, communicate by whispering or sign language if you have to. The sun rises at 06-00hours so I want you all alert by 05-00hours. That's all for now … I'll give further orders then." Before dismissing us he deployed four men to stand guard and keep watch for any sign of terrorist activity.

"Blimey," I thought as I bedded down, "it's alright saying we've been drilled for this … I bloomin' well haven't." I placed my army cloak around my shoulders and parked myself down on a sloping mound of grassland, but I couldn't settle, as once again anxiety started to build up within me. It seemed so unreal that I was actually going into action alongside these courageous infantrymen. "Bloomin' 'eck," I trembled inwardly, "some of us might be killed tomorrow and one of them could be me." My fear intensified when it occurred to me that if we'd acquired data about the terrorists' whereabouts, then they may have received information regarding our coming and could be waiting in readiness to ambush us.

My thoughts wandered back to my childhood when my grandad used to tell me tales of the time he spent in the trenches on the Western Front during the First World War. At that moment I realised how he must have felt on the nights before he went on the offensive against the Germans. I was suddenly brought back to reality.

"Ouch!" I moaned as thousands of ants started to crawl all over me and they bit like hell. Along with my comrades, I had to strip off and douse myself with loads of insect repellant, which thankfully kept them at bay. I didn't get a wink of sleep that night but it wasn't nerves or insects that kept me awake, it was the cold … it was absolutely freezing. "I don't believe this," I muttered through chattering teeth, "I was baking this afternoon and now I'm freezing to death!"

Sure enough, before the crack of dawn the officer ordered us to converge onto the small village and muster all the people together. The soldiers did their job well. After stealthfully negotiating the steep grassy hillside on their backsides they gradually encroached upon the tiny hamlet and took it over without any resistance. After thoroughly searching every hut the troops rounded up the poor unsuspecting natives and herded them together. I hated this part, as adrenaline sent some of the soldiers power crazy, and they savagely prodded the males with the butts of their rifles and aggressively ordered them to lay face down spread-eagled on the ground.

Small frightened bewildered children clung to their mothers' clothing, wondering what was happening ... they were sobbing their hearts out. I felt awful and ashamed as I saw the sheer look of horror on the faces of terrified women, some of whom were bare breasted and holding crying babies in their arms. I'll never forget their petrified expressions as they stood there quaking with fear. Other soldiers bawled loudly and held loaded rifles at the ready, pointing them at the poor inhabitants who obviously thought they were going to die.

I couldn't help but think that I didn't know these soldiers ... they were totally different to the friendly bunch of lads I had grown to know. Their hateful expressions with screwed up eyes and snarling mouths gave off a totally different demeanor. To me they were no longer acting like decent human beings but more like savages, a frenzied mob ... and I was part of it. It seemed deplorable to treat our fellowmen in this manner but I tried to convince myself that it was a necessary evil.

"What am I doing here," I thought, none of these poor souls look like tyrants to me, they're just ordinary families trying to survive the best way they can." During the short spell I'd spent in Africa the Cameroonians had been my friends and here I was helping to round them up like animals in the most appalling and degrading way. A strong feeling of disgust overtook me and I felt sick in the pit of my stomach. It so happened that the soldiers detained four men who turned out to be known terrorists, but even that didn't ease the feeling of guilt that I felt in my heart. Despite the fact that we found some antiquated weapons, I still felt bad about it

As far as the army was concerned the entire operation was a success without one round of ammunition being fired off.

Yet once again my expertise came to the fore as two lads badly needed stitches to deep lacerations in their forearms; and again the cause was elephant grass. One of the lads happened to be the sprog who, after patching him up, became a little friendlier towards me.

As we made our way back to the top of the ridge with the insurgents, who were made to carry the confiscated weapon, the sun had risen revealing a sight to behold. There stretched out in front of me for as far as the eye could see were miles and miles of jungle, which I hadn't been able to detect in the dark. It wasn't the most beautiful sight I'd ever seen, but it was certainly the most unusual as the thick mass of trees swayed in the wind, making ripples like waves on the ocean. Just as the horizon on the Atlantic had looked like the end of the world, so did this ... the only difference was that this ocean was green instead of blue.

After handing the terrorists over to the Nigerian police we made our way back to camp. The first thing I did when I got there was to get rid of the stinking clothes and have a shower.

On returning to my hut, Pius Tashi gave me a warm greeting, "Alright Mr John, it is nice for you to be back."

"And it's good to be back Pius, and nice to see you!"

"Now you rest Mr John while I wash your clothes and clean boots."

"Thank you very much Pius, you're great," I said lying on my bunk. Before I drifted off, I looked up at the corrugated tin roof and felt like I was in heaven.

That was my first taste of a patrol and I have to admit I didn't relish the thought of doing any more. Even so, just like my comrades, during the coming months I had to do my fair share. However, unlike my first experience I didn't have to sleep out in the open anymore. The reason for this was that 'B' Company covered the vast jungle area around Kumba in regions like Tombel and Edibinjok, which were coffee and cocoa plantations. 'B' Company was made up of three platoons, 4, 5 and 6, and usually two platoons would be out on patrol duty whilst the other one guarded the camp. We sometimes kipped down for the night in barns on the plantations but mostly, if we were away from camp for a few days at a time, we billeted in a large fortress-type building in Essosong.

Whilst out with 5 Platoon, Sergeant Bull, a veteran of the Second World War informed me that it was known as a German Schloss. The stone castle, which had been built by the Germans prior to the First World War, now served as a very useful outstation for our lads. It was ideally set up with sleeping quarters and running

91

water and stood in idyllic surroundings. After a hard day's trekking around the jungle it was an ideal retreat and very comforting to return home to. It even had an upstairs section that was bunked out. Because of the home comforts, some of the lads nicknamed it 'Shangri-la'. There was another reason why the lads and I enjoyed it so much.

One of the locals, in his early forties, had the job of warden and kept an eye on the place at all times. He happened to have a couple of daughters and it became apparent to all the lads that he wasn't quite as vigilant with them. His house stood in the middle of a smallholding, about fifty yards from the fortress where he kept chickens, goats and other livestock. It was easily overlooked from the battlements and, much to the amusement of the troops, the two young girls used to sunbathe regularly in scanty bikinis within the garden area and flaunt themselves. Lots of lads would stand on the ramparts from where they had a bird's eye view of the two bathing beauties and wave their shirts in the air. Some of the soldiers would cheer excitedly and make innuendos in an effort to prompt the girls to strip off and bare all. The girls appeared to enjoy the attention bestowed on them and would make certain gestures, which only spurred the lads on even more. The parents of the two youngsters must have known what was going on, because we could plainly see into their dining area where they ate around a large table. To my knowledge nothing more went on, but this simple display used to send the lads wild. At night time it was certainly a talking point over a can of lager and, without a doubt, was good for morale.

During the coming months the outpost proved to be very efficient, and whilst I was with 'B' Company, the troops successfully policed the surrounding areas, and arrested many terrorists, illegal immigrants and smugglers. On one mission alone my Burnley mate, Martin Grogan, went on patrol from this fortress with 5 Platoon who, along with some Nigerian policemen, took over a terrorist's camp and arrested at least twenty suspected terrorists. The camp was ingenious and self sufficient in every aspect, housing livestock and growing food products. Due to careful planning and skillful tactics, the infantry lads easily overtook the camp with little resistance and within a short time had rounded up all the renegades. Once in custody, the terrorists toed the line and didn't make any attempt to escape, as they knew full well that the Nigerian police wouldn't think twice about shooting them dead on the spot if they so much as blinked.

On routine patrols the infantry did their own policing with the help of a native tracker. Whilst I was out with them, we sometimes came across some locals doing a bit of poaching simply to survive; but the officer in charge usually let the pitiful blokes off with a caution, knowing full well that if he handed them over to the Nigerian police the unfortunate men would be in big trouble. This really proved to me that the squad was only seeking the real offenders and it eased my conscience somewhat.

On one occasion we came across a camp with a few deserted huts, which contained many knives, spears, makeshift swords, blow pipes with poison arrows and some primitive guns. After destroying the camp the weapons were confiscated and shared out amongst the men as souvenirs.

Working close to the border crossing we often came across French colonial troops patrolling the French side. They always appeared to be a mean bunch of blaggards equipped with bandoliers and camouflaged gear. We could only communicate with them using sign language from our side of a river but we never ever crossed over the border. We didn't feel totally at ease when we were in their near vicinity, as there was something untoward about them. Our senior NCOs, veterans of the Second World War, warned us that they were nasty pieces of work and ordered us to keep a strict vigil and be doubly alert. There were lots of inhabitants being murdered on the French side and we suspected that the French troops were the culprits, who then laid the blame on others. If any terrorists fell into their trap there was no mercy shown, and most were shot dead there and then. Even if their prisoners were only suspected terrorists it didn't seem to make any difference; their chance of survival was very slim … life seemed to be so cheap. There was definitely something improper about those French troops.

After a full day's patrolling of the jungle in the sweltering heat it was always good to get back to the German fortress; it was a sight for sore eyes. The lads loved nothing more than to get a few beers down their throats and talk about the day's happenings and then finish up with a sing-song. They were truly courageous devoted men, professional in every way, but at the end of the day this was their way of letting off steam and relaxing. Along with a few other lads, Martin and I loved to sunbathe within the grounds of the old fortress during our off duty time.

Upon returning to Kumba I exchanged experiences with my colleagues regarding different incidents, and they all had similar tales to tell. We all came to the same conclusion that the French troops were ruthless.

Overall, my workmates seemed to prefer going out on patrols to nursing duties, but I personally felt much more at home and at ease working within the confines of the hospital.

****

Regimental Colours.

R A M C
Faithful in Adversity.

95

Plymouth Hoe.

Seaton Barracks.

Big Bri with RAMC friends.

Plymouth Days.

Bri and Ernie Christie.

Relaxing around the
ponies on Dartmoor.

Devonshire.

Rob & me on the deck
of the *Devonshire.*

Rob by the rails of
the mighty ship.

Dug Smith (middle) & his mates
relaxing on deck.

Dug by the rails

Sunbathing on deck of
Devonshire.

Sighting of another majestic ship

Devonshire anchored up at Victoria.

Four Barrow lads en-route to the Cameroons, on board the troopship Devonshire
L. to R. Alan Parkinson, Brian Dempster, Billy Kell and Pete Maguire

Above L to R. Geoff Stubbs, Eric Shaw
Middle: Alan Parkinson Ronnie Phair
Front. Ralph Morgan

Above L to R Ted Hughes, Unknown, Unknown
Front Alan Parkinson

Onboard the Devonshire en-route to the Cameroons September 1960

Life on the ocean waves.

Making a living from boats.

Local natives bartering their wares with the lads on the *Devonshire* from small boats when we dropped anchor at Victoria.

Typical jungle roads around Kumba.
*(Photo taken from the back of the leading
3-ton Bedford truck).*

3 ton Bedford truck driving through a small Kumba
village.

Me, Nelson, Spud Murphy and Rob.

Jungle clearing to make way for a road.

Local bar.

Big Bri below, associating with the local help.

Rob and me trekking
through Elephant
Grass.

Rob and me having fun
at the Blue Lagoon.

Above: Me and Big Bri larking about.
Note; The shiny boots.

Left: Rob and me trekking through elephant grass on our way to the Blue Lagoon.

B Company, No 5 Platoon relaxing in between patrols at Essong Outstation. Sergeant Bull in prominent position above the number 5 poster.

Essosong Outstation, a German fortress built prior to the First World War. 1914 -1918.
Used by B Company as an outpost during patrols - a very cosy retreat after a hard day's trekking in the jungle.
Nicknamed by some of the lads as Shangri-la.

Cameroons Vs B Company.
Martin is the first soldier stood up on the left. Does anyone
recognise themselves?
Note: One Cameroon player with only one boot on – one player in
his bare feet.
The scoreline finished at 2-2 ... a great game!
Below: An actual cutting taken from the *News Of The World*
newspaper on the day that England played Cameroons in the 1990
quarter finals of the World Cup.

Snatch of the day! We beat the rest to the BIG game

ENGLAND 22
CAMEROON 11

That's how many
boots they wore
at our last match

UPON MY SOLE! The Cameroon team, with only 11 boots to go round, pose with England in 1961. But they may have us on the run tonight with full footwear

JUNGLE drums beat out a staggering
scoreline the first time England played
Cameroon . . . "Us 2 Dem 2."
For those World Cup wizards from West
Africa won an amazing DRAW when the
two countries clashed in a forest clearing.
And the parrots that screeched in the treetops
weren't half as sick as our lads after the match—

Team trooped
out with only

What can you get for
around a £1 nowadays?

112

I can't take these jungle roads any more.

Church just over the bridge from Kumba in the French
Cameroon's, where I bought my Roman Catholic Missal.

Martin patrolling through Elephant Grass.

Above: Rob on patrol with his medical bag.

Right: Big Bri displaying a Stirling machine gun.

Monkeying
around at
Kumba Camp.

On patrol with a local native tracker.

Taking a break on patrol.

Above: Out on patrol with a native tracker.

Right: Even the Nigerian police need to rest.

Troops having a breather whilst patrolling with a tracker and the Nigerian police. Martin having a swig from his water

At least 20 bandits captured by B Company, 5 Platoon, during a raid on a main terrorists' camp.
Martin can clearly be seen standing by the side of a Nigerian policeman.
Note how innocent the natives look!

B Company, No 5 platoon escorting captured insurgents back to base.   Note: A good shot of the SLR rifle.

Guns at the ready. B Company, 5 Platoon, alongside Nigerian Police, marching prisoners back to base.

A serious and tired looking members of the Anti-Tank platoon, taking a breather during a route march in the early days at Bamenda. I am third from the left on the front row. The two lads facing the camera are Alan Welsh left and John Rennie right.

Alan Parkinson's photographs.

The mortar platoon on patrol being led by the pistol Lt Olsen who later was awarded the Queens Commendation for leading his platoon in an attack on a terrorist camp George Day a Barrow lad is the Corporal in the second line holding a sterling Sub machine gun

121

Above Yours truly, patrolling out of Sante Coffee in
the Magga region photo taken by Cpl Mckelvie

Above Keith Hindle from Clitheroe and Myself
Bamenda Camp New Years day 1961

Alan
Parkinson

122

Haul of weapons confiscated during the patrol led by Lieutenant Olson, as described in Alan Parkinson's account (chapter six).

The German built fortress at Essosong

Looking down from the battlements onto the
warden's smallholding and the grounds where
the two beauties used to sunbathe.

Medic's hut. *Can you spot me?*

FAITHFUL
IN
ADVERSITY

Overlooking the Blue Lagoon.

The Blue Lagoon.
Note: The floating platform – lower left.

Above: Bill Hupboard, Mark Radiven and me with our working colleagues at Kumba Camp. The letters A M are part of a RAMC sign made out of bamboos.

Below are children from around the camp in their living environment.

Note the typical pot bellies on the children, caused by malnutrition.

Spud Murphy and lads showing affection to the local Kumba children.

Local fun.

Above: Bathtime.

Below: Schoolchildren.

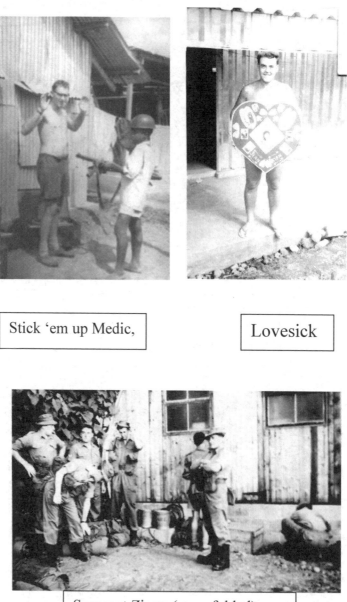

Stick 'em up Medic,

Lovesick

Sergeant Ziggy (arms folded)
with some of the lads.

Sergeant Ziggy, Big Bri, Johnny Church
and others climbing Mount Cameroon.

Big Bri off duty.

MARKET DAY.

Cattle for the slaughter

Butcher chopping up meat.

Ladies boutique

Buying a shirt.

Market gathering.

Nurse on duty.

Anyone for horse riding

Bri and Johnny Church.
Note: Boy carrying basket on his
head.

Sergeant Ziggy struggling though elephant grass.

Hospitals

Hospital Flood.

First Aid Demonstration.

Buea Army Hospital

Tiko Hospital

River Patrol

Me resting on the bank of a Bamenda river on my way from Mamfe to Kumba.

Explorer

Posh part of Buea.

Lads having a few beers with the locals.

School time

Above: Howard Fanshaw relaxing by the side of the racecourse at Bamenda camp.
Below: Native huts around Bamenda Camp. The race course can be seen just to the right.

Above: Howard, Signals, displaying sophisticated radio equipment during a regimental parade at Bamenda Camp.
Below: A rather sophisticated canon.

Santa Customs Outpost.

Washing facilities at the outpost.

Being checked through customs.

Home Sweet Home.

Socialising with the locals.

Fancy a dip?

Hang out the washing
on the Seigfield Line

Haircut time.

Stretcher Rover used by medics.

Bamenda Camp.

Hello little fella.

Modern technology in radio

Fiesta Day.

Neville Atkinson,
Howard Fanshaw
and mates.

Leisure time.

Watch this lads.

Swimming pool created by
the advanced party of engineers.

Outlying mountains and road to camp.

Bamenda Terrain.

Savannah upland.

Good friends

Anyone for Pinyin?

Above: Target practice in the Savannah Uplands.

Below: Baby carrier.

Me and Mark Radiven outside the Bamenda
Hospital with our native workers.
The girl next to me is Lucy.

Above: Cattle Drive.

Below: Easter Period.

Above: Howard, Signals.
Below: Campsite.

Homeward Bound.

Above: Scenery around Mount Cameroon.

Below: Small boats in Buea area.

Jungle Rivers

On the way home.
Loaded up and ready to go.

Going Home

DEVONSHIRE, portside.

Above:
Devonshire –
what a beautiful
sight!

Left: Docking
at Gran Canarias
on the way
home.

168

Top: Howard, Neville and mate on Gran Canarias Beach.
Below: Others taking advantage of the mini break.

Blighty here we come.

Ship passing on the starboard side.

Homeward bound.

RULES

This certificate is valid only if the vaccine has been approved by the World Health Organisation and if the vaccinating centre has been designated by the health administration for the territory in which that centre is situated.

The validity of this certificate shall extend for a period of six years, beginning ten days after the date of vaccination or, in the event of a revaccination within such period of six years, from the date of that revaccination.

Any amendment of this certificate, or erasure, or failure to complete any part of it, may render it invalid.

Ce certificat n'est valable que si le vaccin employé a été approuvé par l'Organisation Mondiale de la Santé et si le centre de vaccination a été habilité par l'administration sanitaire du territoire dans lequel ce centre est situé.

La validité de ce certificat couvre une période de six ans commençant dix jours après la date de la vaccination ou, dans le cas d'une revaccination au cours de cette période de six ans, le jour de cette revaccination.

Toute correction ou rature sur le certificat ou l'omission d'une quelconque des mentions qu'il comporte peut affecter sa validité.

ARMY
DOCUMENTS

Form of certificate prescribed by the International Sanitary Regulations.

INTERNATIONAL CERTIFICATE OF VACCINATION
OR REVACCINATION AGAINST YELLOW FEVER

CERTIFICAT INTERNATIONAL DE VACCINATION
OU DE REVACCINATION CONTRE LA FIÈVRE JAUNE

{ This is to certify that }
{ Je soussigné(e) certifie que }

{ Number } **23633187** { Rank } *pre*
{ Numéro } { Grade }

{ Name } **COWELL** "
{ nom }

{ Date of birth } **11-4-39** { sex } **MALE**
{ né(e) le } { sexe }

{ whose signature follows }
{ dont la signature suit }

has on the date indicated overleaf been vaccinated or revaccinated against yellow fever.

a été vacciné(e) ou revacciné(e) contre la fièvre jaune à la date indiquée au verso.

IMPORTANT : See the Rules on the back.

Vaccinations against Yellow Fever & Smallpox.

RULES

The validity of this certificate shall extend for a period of three years, beginning eight days after the date of a successful primary vaccination or, in the event of a revaccination, on the date of that revaccination (see Note I below).

The approved stamp mentioned overleaf must be in a form prescribed by the health administration of the territory in which the vaccination is performed (see Note 2 below).

Any amendment of this certificate, or erasure, or failure to complete any part of it, may render it invalid.

La validité de ce certificat couvre une période de trois ans commençant huit jours après la date de la primovaccination effectuée avec succès (prise) ou, dans le cas d'une revaccination, le jour de cette revaccination.

Le cachet d'authentification doit être conforme au modèle prescrit par l'administration sanitaire du territoire où la vaccination est effectuée.

Toute correction ou rature sur le certificat ou l'omission d'une quelconque des mentions qu'il comporte peut affecter sa validité.

NOTES

1. Method of Dating.

Misunderstandings have arisen as to the date of issue, and therefore the period of validity, of International Certificates of Vaccination, due to differences in national or other practice of recording dates : for example, the 10th August, 1957, may be written as 10 Aug., 1957, or Aug. 10, 1957, or 10.8.1957.

These misunderstandings can be avoided if dates on International Certificates are always written thus :—

the day should be placed first in **Arabic** numerals ;
the month should appear second in **letters** ;
the year should come last in **Arabic** numerals.

The above example would then appear as " 10 August, 1957."

2. Approved Stamp.

Approved stamps have been prescribed for the United Kingdom. If the vaccinator is not himself an authorised user of a stamp, the person vaccinated must take or send the certificate for stamping to a Local Authority.

In England and Wales, this is the Town Council, Urban District Council or Rural District Council, and in Scotland the Council of the County or large Burgh, in whose area the vaccinator practises.

For Northern Ireland, see the Notice to Travellers issued by the Ministry of Health and Local Government, Belfast.

830236 Wt.65077-2585 500M 5/58 Gp.789 F. & C. Ltd.

**Form of certificate prescribed by the International
Sanitary Regulations.** (Art 99)

INTERNATIONAL CERTIFICATE OF VACCINATION
OR REVACCINATION AGAINST SMALLPOX

CERTIFICAT INTERNATIONAL DE VACCINATION
OU DE REVACCINATION CONTRE LA VARIOLE

{ This is to certify that }
{ Je soussigné(e) certifie que }

{ number } **23633183** { rank } Pte
{ numéro } { grade }

{ name } **COWELL J.W.**
{ nom }

{ date of birth } **11 Apr 39** { sex } Male
{ né(e) le } { sexe }

{ whose signature follows }
{ dont la signature suit }

has on the date indicated overleaf been vaccinated or revaccinated against smallpox.

a été vacciné(e) ou revacciné(e) contre la variole à la date indiquée au verso.

IMPORTANT : See the Rules and Notes on the back.
This certificate, if folded along the central vertical line, can be kept in a passport (with a rubber band).

FOLD HERE

NOTICE TO BE GIVEN TO A MAN COMPLETING SERVICE
IN THE REGULAR, RESERVE, OR AUXILIARY FORCES
WHO WILL BECOME A MAN OF THE ARMY RESERVE
UNDER THE NAVY, ARMY AND AIR FORCE RESERVES
ACTS, 1954 AND 1959. 1964

To :

No. 2363 3183   Rank   PTE.   Surname   COWELL

Christian or   JOHN WILLIAM.   Regt./   RAMC
Fore Name(s)   Corps

You are hereby notified that on completing your engagement of   PART TIME
SERVICE   in the   RAMC/AER   you will become a member of
the Army Reserve, Class I (Army General Reserve) by virtue of the provisions of the Navy,
Army and Air Force Reserves Acts, 1954 and 1959, and that, unless previously discharged
from that Reserve, you will remain a member of that Reserve until 30th June, 1969 or until
you attain the age of forty-five years, whichever is the earlier.

You are hereby warned that as a man of the Army General Reserve you will be subject
to the following liabilities :—

(1) To be called out on permanent service by proclamation of Her Majesty in Council
under Section 5 of the Army Reserve Act, 1950, in case of imminent national danger
or great emergency ; when so called out you will be liable to serve in the United
Kingdom or elsewhere.

(2) To be called out on permanent service by the direction of a Secretary of State
under Section 6 (1) (a) of the Army Reserve Act, 1950, for service at any place
in the United Kingdom in defence of the United Kingdom against actual or
apprehended attack.

*(3) To notify to the authority stated within fourteen days of being required to do so
by notice in writing sent to you by or on behalf of the Army Council, your name
and address and certain particulars relating to your occupation or qualifications
which will be specified in the notice.

You will not be liable to be called out in aid of the civil
power under Section 10 of the Army Reserve Act, 1950, nor   Official Stamp
for any form of training.

You will not be entitled to receive any pay during your
service in the Army General Reserve unless you are called
out on permanent service.

*You are requested to inform the Officer in charge of
Record Office of any change in your permanent address.

Notice of mobilisation.

Demobilisation Certificate.

NOTICE FOR POSTING FOR MOBILIZATION
(Regular and Army Emergency Reserves only)

You are NOT required to rejoin until you are told to do
so. (See Instructions below.)

Army No. 2363 31 83   Rank. PTE

Name   Cowell   J.W.

Regt./Corps   R.A.M.C.

In a national emergency, certain selected reservists would
be required to join for service IMMEDIATELY and without
waiting for the NOTICE TO JOIN THE ARMY FOR
PERMANENT SERVICE (Army Form D463)—see Part II
of the Reservist's Instruction Book.
ON THE PUBLICATION OF A GOVERNMENT
ANNOUNCEMENT (WHETHER BY NEWSPAPER,
POSTER OR BROADCAST) CALLING-OUT RESERVISTS
HOLDING THIS NOTICE OF POSTING YOU WILL
IMMEDIATELY COMPLY WITH THE INSTRUCTIONS
IN PART II OF YOUR RESERVIST'S INSTRUCTION BOOK
USING THIS NOTICE OF POSTING AS A NOTICE
TO JOIN AND REPORT TO
B. A. O. R.   REINFORCEMENTS

DEPOT   Q.T.E. & HQ AER R.A.M.C.   Unit

LOGH BARRACKS, MYTCHETT, (place of joining)

ASH VALE (nearest railway station)

RECORD OFFICE
WINCHESTER

Date   1 APRIL 63

READ ALSO THE INSTRUCTIONS ON THE BACK OF THIS FORM.

Medals, Clasps, Decorations, Mentions in Despatches
Any special acts of gallantry or distinguished conduct
brought to notice in Brigade or superior orders:—

Army Form B108D

Certificate of Service

Health Warning.

IMPORTANT NOTICE TO PERSONS ARRIVING FROM ABROAD	AVIS IMPORTANT AUX PERSONNES ARRIVANT DE L'ÉTRANGER	BELANGRIJKE WAARSCHUWING AAN PERSONEN KOMENDE UIT HET BUITENLAND
Whilst abroad you may, without knowing it, have been in contact with some dangerous epidemic disease such as smallpox or typhus. If during the next 21 days—wherever you may be—you or any person living in the same house fall ill, ill, in your own interest call in a doctor immediately and give him this card. NOTE.—Whilst in the United Kingdom, you will not be charged for this visit by the doctor if you ask for his services under the National Health Service and he agrees to this.	Pendant votre séjour à l'étranger, vous avez pu, à votre insu, vous trouver en contact avec une maladie contagieuse dangereuse, notamment la variole ou le typhus exanthématique. Si dans les 21 jours qui suivent, quel que soit le lieu où vous vous trouvez, vous-même ou toute personne vivant dans la même maison que vous, tombez malade, dans votre propre intérêt, appelez aussitôt un médecin et remettez-lui la présente carte. NOTE.—Pendant votre séjour au Royaume-Uni si vous demandez au médecin de bénéficier du " National Health Service " et qu'il accepte, il ne vous réclamera pas d'honoraires pour cette visite.	Tijdens Uw verblijf in de vreemde, kunt U, zonder het te weten, in aanraking zijn geweest met personen die besmet waren met een gevaarlijke ziekte die aldaar voorkomt, b.v. pokken of vlektyphus. Indien U of iemand anders, die zich in hetzelfde huis bevindt, in de komende 21 dagen ziek mocht worden, raadpleeg dan in Uw eigen belang onmiddellijk een dokter, waar U zich ook bevindt en stel hem deze kaart ter hand. N.B.—Indien, tijdens Uw verblijf in het Verenigd Koninkrijk, U de hulp van een dokter inroept, wordt U deze voor dit bezoek gratis verleend onder de " National Health Service ", mits de dokter hiermede instemt.
NOTICE TO DOCTOR CALLED TO A PERSON RECENTLY ARRIVED FROM ABROAD The holder of this card arrived at the place and on the date stated on the front. It is possible that he may be suffering from some acute infectious disease not normally present in this country. Smallpox should be particularly borne in mind as the rash may be modified by previous vaccination. If you suspect any such illness please notify the Medical Officer of Health at once by telephone.	**AVIS AU MÉDECIN APPELÉ AUPRÈS D'UNE PERSONNE RECEMMENT ARRIVÉE DE L'ÉTRANGER** Le porteur de cette carte est arrivé au lieu et à la date indiqués au verso. Il est possible qu'il soit atteint d'une maladie contagieuse qui normalement n'existe pas dans ce pays. Il convient particulièrement de penser à la variole, car l'apparence de l'éruption peut être modifiée du fait d'une vaccination antérieure. Si vous avez quelque raison de suspecter une maladie de ce genre, veuillez en aviser aussitôt l'autorité sanitaire compétente.	**RAAD AAN DE GENEESKUNDIGE ONTBODEN BIJ EEN ZIEKE DIE KORTGELEDEN IS AANGEKOMEN UIT HET BUITENLAND** De houder van deze kaart is op de voorkantvermelde plaats en datum aangekomen. Het is mogelijk, dat hij aan een besmettelijke ziekte lijdt, welke hier te lande niet inheems is. Bijzondere aandacht dient te worden besteed aan de mogelijkheid van pokken. De aard van de uitslag kan door een vroegere vaccinatie gewijzigd worden. Indien U een dergelijke ziekte vaststelt of vermoedt, wordt U verzocht met de meeste spoed de geneeskundige instantie te waarschuwen bij wie U de besmettelijke ziekten aangeeft.

WESTERN EUROPEAN UNION
IMPORTANT NOTICE

UNION DE L'EUROPE OCCIDENTALE
AVIS IMPORTANT

WEST-EUROPESE UNIE
BELANGRIJKE WAARSCHUWING

ISSUED IN THE UNITED KINGDOM BY

MINISTRY OF HEALTH, LONDON
DEPARTMENT OF HEALTH FOR SCOTLAND, EDINBURGH
MINISTRY OF HEALTH AND LOCAL GOVERNMENT, BELFAST

Form Port 16

PLACE AND DATE
OF ARRIVAL

LIEU ET DATE
D'ARRIVÉE

PLAATS EN DATUM
VAN AANKOMST

PROPER OFFICER
CUSTOMS & EXCISE
30 APR 1961
STANSTED AIRPORT,
ESSEX.

Back in Civvy Street.

Peter Spedding and me during our nursing training alongside a load of beauties.

Just ready for work over the Christmas period.

Brian and Jean
in their
courting days.

Recent photo
sporting my
Medic's Badge.

Old mates from the Cameroons.

My old buddie Bri.

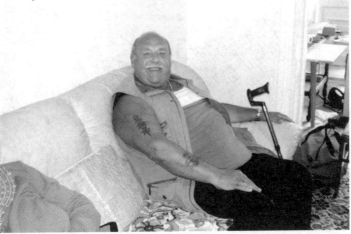

Rob, Martin, Duggie.
Howard, Brian.
Neville, John.

Seven Cameroon mates.

Me, Martin and Neville

The Roman Missal that I purchased on New Years Day 1961 from the Catholic Missionary that lay over the bridge in the French Cameroons.
I had it signed by the missionaries at Kumba on that day, and later at the Mankon Diocese of Bamenda.

A regimental Christmas card that I sent to my mum.

Map of the Cameroons.
I like this map as it shows all the places that I visited.
Victoria, where the *Devonshire* docked.
Tiko, the site of the civilian hospital.
Buea, the main camp based at the foot of Mount Cameroon.
Kumba, my first camp where I did most of my patrolling and field hospital work,
which was based about 50 miles inland in thick jungle territory.
Bamenda, my second camp set a further 150 miles north in mountainous countryside where I spent most of my time at outposts.
Finally the notorious Mamfe Airforce base where the RAF personnel were very anti-social

CHAPTER FIVE
THE WORLD CUP

I enjoyed both working alongside the happy contented inhabitants and intermingling with them on the market and other places; they lived in impoverished conditions, but would gladly have given the shirts off their backs in a crisis. One thing that stood out because of their hand to mouth existence, was that all the natives, including the children, had large pot bellies with grotesque belly buttons due to malnutrition. Because of the shortage of food the bairns were forever foraging around the camp site begging for something to eat. I, along with my colleagues, used to pass them food through the wire fence surrounding the camp; this was strictly against army policy, but the lads did it anyway. But then again, how could we refuse the poor little blighters as they stood there like ragamuffins with their little appealing faces.

Despite their plight these little ones had an ever beaming smile, displaying pearly white teeth. It took me back to my childhood when I, along with my mates, used to stand outside Burnley Fire Station and scrounge meat pies and cakes. But this was far more serious because, although I was brought up in poverty, we were always assured of at least one good meal a day. It might have only been a school dinner but it was nourishing and sustaining, whereas these poor souls could go for days, or maybe weeks without having a proper meal.

We soldiers were well fed on the camp and lots of food was wasted and used as pig swill in the same way as it was in schools back home. It got me to thinking just how much these youngsters would appreciate what we were throwing away. I didn't actually collect anything from the pig swill, but I did collect remnants left over on plates such as pies, potatoes and bread. Besides feeding the food through the wire fence, we sometimes used to give it to Pius Tashi, our hut boy, who appreciated it immensely.

Despite their fate of being born in squalour and having to follow in the same footsteps as their parents' impoverished existence, the young ones always appeared happy. I know they didn't know anything different and seemed to accept their lot as normal, but I couldn't help but compare them with children of the same ages as kids back home. It made my blood boil to think of all the money that was being spent on armaments and defence, not just by my own country, but by the Cameroon Government as well. It came across as clear as crystal that the powers that be didn't give a damn about these poor people.

The Yoruba women did most of the home chores and could readily be seen carrying large water containers balanced precariously on their heads, never spilling a drop. The scene reminded me of the song that Harry Bellafonte used to sing:

Oh island in the sun
Willed to me by my father's hand,
All my days I will live in praise
Of your forest's waters and shining sand.
I see woman on bended knee
Cutting cane for her family,
I see man by the water side
Catching fish by the rising tide.

As the women went about their daily tasks it seemed as though the song had been written especially about them.

The men were more into sport, especially football, which had been instilled into them from an early age. Young boys cheerfully played on dirt tracks using a small rubber ball the size of a tennis ball … and good they were too. Many a time I enjoyed watching them play competitively, adeptly using skills I'd never seen before.

As it happened, Pete and I enjoyed playing the game and, as there were some decent players amongst the infantry mob, we formed teams and played against each other. Martin Grogan was an exceptional player, much better than I was, so he was always guaranteed a game. I'd played alongside him back home in Burnley during my teenage years for Sandygate Youth Club. Being a natural player and a prolific goal scorer, he'd always been an automatic choice in the youth team, whereas I'd spent many hours as a reserve.

Out here in Africa, history seemed to be repeating itself, as once again I participated in many matches solely on the sidelines. Word of the football games spread through the camp and some of the native workers asked if they could join in. After a few sessions the reputation of our football team spread further afield and ultimately the village council approached the camp, inviting us to play against their local team. We all eagerly accepted and looked forward to the challenge, but I was in for a disappointment … of all the days, I happened to be on duty. I certainly wouldn't have got into the team but I would have loved to watch the game. On the other hand, Martin and Pete were both obvious choices and went to the match with a smile on their faces. I was unhappy about missing the occasion, but all the same when the lads got back after the game Martin gave me a running commentary. The Cameroon team was made up from specially selected players from various towns and villages within the region, and nearly four-thousand spectators turned up from far and wide to watch their squad play a team of super fit soldiers. What a spectacle it had been. Our team had been rather complacent about the whole affair, taking it for granted that the match would be a walkover, but what an awakening they got.

On the day of the match our lads turned up in a Bedford truck equipped out with two nets, two football strips, an assortment of football boots and some buckets and sponges. Taking into account that they were playing a team of comparison to a county team back home in England, the lads expected to play on a top-notch pitch. But it was not to be … the playing field was more like a building site in a forest clearing with potholes everywhere; the goal posts and the bar were cut from thickets, and the dressing room was a cluster of banana trees. But the biggest shock of all was the Cameroon's football strip; our side ran onto the pitch wearing blue and white kits, but the natives lined up in shorts and … nothing else. Not one of the eleven players had a pair of football boots between them … they stood there ready to take us on in their bare feet.

"I can't believe this," quipped Martin, "how can they possibly expect to play against us with nowt on their feet ... we'll murder 'em."

All our lads started laughing and wanted to call the game off but the natives wouldn't have it.

"No no, we play ... we give you plenty good game."

The local inhabitants were adamant, pointing out that they always played in their bare feet.

"But some of you are bound to get injured," said Pete.

"Yeah," agreed Martin, "our lads will be doing a lot of sliding tackles and the studded boots could easily crush a foot ... u-ugh, especially a bare one."

"That's right, it doesn't bear thinking about," our captain butted in, "some of your lads could be maimed."

Still the natives remained insistent, "No, no," said their spokesperson, "we be alright, we play plenty times against teams with boots."

The rest of the Cameroon team started chanting cheekily, "You afraid we win," adding, "we take care not to hurt you."

Their persistence and determination to play prevailed and so the game got underway; but first of all our lads got together and mustered up a red strip and five pairs of football boots.

"There's an odd boot here," said Martin as he rumbled through the back of the truck.

"An odd boot's no good," quipped Pete, "they can't do anything with that?" He couldn't have been more wrong.

As we handed over the trivial gift, the Kumba team expressed their delight by hugging all the soldiers.

"Now with boots we beat you easily," they grinned impudently as they ran back to the banana trees.

"I don't know why they're so happy," said Pete, "they still need another six pairs. Anyway, I wonder which players will wear the boots."

"Probably the forwards," replied Martin.

"I think the defenders will wear them to help them tackle better." responded Pete.

They were both wrong, but what a laugh everybody got.

186

As the Kumba lads paraded onto the pitch three of them were wearing a pair of boots, but five of them wore just one boot each.

"Bloomin' 'eck," laughed Martin, "that's the funniest thing I've ever seen in my life ... I can't believe it!"

"No neither can I," roared Pete, "it's hilarious. Anyway come on, let's get out there and wop 'em."

Any preconceptions our lads had about the game before it started were soon quashed and they were under no illusions by the end of it. The courageous natives threw themselves into the game pouncing like tigers for every ball. Boots or no boots, they weren't afraid of going in for a tackle.

But despite their determination, with only five minutes of the game gone, Martin took a good cross from the right wing and scored a brilliant header. Not to be outdone, the Cameroonians fought back and within minutes they equalised. Joyous shouts resounded through the air accompanied by the loud beating of drums and squeaking parrots. The game continued, but despite every team member playing with sheer determination, the score remained at 1-1 after forty-five minutes.

At the break, visibly shaken, our squad knew they had a tough second half on their hands.

"Right lads," said our captain, "no more complacency ... let's get out there and give it to 'em!"

The Cameroonians took the restart and the clash of the titans continued. Both sides were in deadlock, but with fifteen minutes to go Martin scored his second putting us into the lead once again; but on this occasion it was a rather scrappy affair. He was in the penalty area with his back to goal surrounded by a cluster of players but somehow niftily he back heeled the ball through the goalkeeper's legs. For the next fourteen minutes the Kumba lads pressed on hungry for an equaliser, but found themselves up against a sturdy defence. Our lads thought that Martin's goal was the match winner but the Cameroon lads had other ideas and scored again with a minute to go. The whistle blew for fulltime with a fair 2-2 scoreline ... what a game! Everyone concerned thoroughly enjoyed it.

Some of our lads were disappointed with the outcome but they soon perked up when an official photographer arrived to take a picture for the county newspaper.

Martin stood up at the end of the second row, whilst two Kumba lads sat on the front row in their bare feet. The photograph turned out brilliant, capturing all the players and many spectators. Martin treasured that picture, and rightly so, not realising that years later in July 1990, Cameroon would be playing England in the quarter finals of the 'World Cup', and that very snapshot would be printed in a national newspaper, showing both teams stood side-by-side ... boots an' all, or ... no boots an' all.

The all important World Cup quarter final match was played on a Sunday evening, but just a week previous there had been a write-up in the 'News of the World' newspaper stating that England would be playing against Cameroons for the first time in the history of football. Martin wasn't having any of that and so contacted the newspaper with living proof, telling them of the original game and the photograph. They were very interested in the story and sent a reporter to Martin's house. After going over all the details and scrutinizing the photo, the editor was highly delighted with the article and decided to print a piece in their next issue.

Sure enough on the morning of the momentous occasion, they displayed the photo across the full breadth of the page and the headlines read **'England 22 – Cameroons 11'**. The printout went on to say how a British Army team had played the Africans way back in 1960 and how the natives had only eleven boots between them. It stated that the international match was to be played that evening and the odds were well stacked in England's favour.

England sported a formidable team with players like David Platt, Paul Gascoigne and Gary Lineker in their squad. In the previous round against Belgium, Platt had scored a brilliant last minute winning goal in extra time by volleying the ball into the top corner of the net, leaving the goalkeeper with no chance. It was a superb strike due to the creative inspiration of Gascoigne, who took a free kick from the left wing, floating the ball perfectly for Platt to connect. The England squad was on top form and now quoted as outright favourites to go through to the semi-finals. Despite everything, Martin pointed out to the newspaper reporter that it wouldn't be an easy game by any means ... his prediction was spot on.

Excitement reached its height and that night loyal supporters sat glued to their television sets. Ironically, after ninety minutes of play the score was 2-2, exactly the same as the original game back in Kumba.

First of all England went in front as David Platt made it 1-0 and it looked as though they were going to cruise home. But then Cameroon moved up a gear, and scored two cracking goals to take the lead. The score remained at 2-1 for a period and with only eight minutes to go England looked in serious trouble. Then fate took a hand as Gary Lineker was brought down in the penalty area. To the delight of England supporters a penalty was awarded and Lineker, England's faithful striker calmly converted the spot kick to level terms. The score remained at 2-2 until the final whistle, taking the game into extra time. During the next thirty minutes the game remained tight but England finally came out on top and won 3-2. However, the winning goal didn't come from open play, as once again, Lineker was brought down in the penalty area. Much to his credit, the England forward yet again slotted the ball neatly into the back of the net. The 3-2 win put England through to the semi finals, which was the best progress they'd made since winning the World Cup in 1966. The victory put every England supporter into a state of ecstasy, fully aware that they had just beaten a brilliant team ... the game certainly put Cameroon on the map. From being a country relatively unknown it was now renowned and applauded worldwide.

****

Meanwhile, back in Africa after the photograph session we regularly played every Saturday afternoon, creating a bond and a friendly atmosphere between the Cameroonians and the troops.

Martin and Pete played against Kumba and other outlying villages many times, whereas I only participated in one game; but I thoroughly enjoyed the match. Our opponents were on form and within twenty minutes we were 2-0 down. But two minutes later Martin scored a cracker, calmly slotting the ball into the bottom corner of the net after taking on the keeper, and five minutes later he levelled the score with a bullet header from a corner kick. At 2-2 the game remained evenly balanced, but just before half-time Kumba's centre forward scored a brilliant goal, putting the Cameroons in front once again. After receiving a perfect cross from the right wing, he controlled it on his chest, then dribbled skillfully past two defenders and slotted the ball into the bottom left hand corner, leaving our goalkeeper helplessly stranded. Along with my teammates I just stood there in disbelief as about two hundred local supporters jumped up and down screaming with delight. We pressed on but at half-time were trailing by one goal.

In the second half we piled on the pressure but just couldn't score. Time was running out and we'd almost given up, but then on the eightieth minute we had a stroke of luck. Pete ran down the right wing and then crossed a perfect ball towards me, but just as I was about to connect the goalkeeper fisted it away from my head. Luckily the ball bobbled on a rough piece of ground and bounced perfectly for Martin, who took the opportunity and skillfully lobbed it over the head of the oncoming goalkeeper for his hat-trick. This stirred up the Kumba lads making them more determined than ever to get the winner ... they were a breed of their own and I couldn't help but admire their unrelenting desire to win combined with a sense of fair play. Nevertheless, they didn't score again and neither did we ... once again the game finished up as a draw.

"By 'eck," said Martin as we walked off the pitch, "I really enjoyed that game."

"I'll bet you did," I laughed, "so would I have done if I'd scored a hat trick."

****

I didn't work alongside Martin but we socialised together along with other friends in the NAAFI and often went swimming in the Blue Lagoon. Like me, Martin enjoyed sport, an odd drink and got stuck into his work, and he also had a stubborn streak, which landed him in trouble now and again. But on one occasion he got three days' jankers for the pettiest offence I ever came across. Although he loved playing football he was never keen on basketball. As it happened, Sergeant Bull, so nicknamed because of his bulky physique, was promoting the game. Two nets had been assembled in the middle of the camp and the burly sergeant was determined to form a squad of fine players. He was aware of Martin's ability on the football field and wanted him as a player in his basketball team. Martin wouldn't have minded so much but it meant that he missed out on playing football, which infuriated him. This was never more so than one Saturday afternoon when Sergeant Bull had a match arranged against another squad that he was determined to win. Martin was an automatic choice.

"But Sergeant," he protested, "I hate basketball, and anyway what about the football team, they've got a game on this afternoon?"

"Forget the blasted football team Grogan," bellowed the sergeant towering over Martin, "you'll play basketball and like it!"

Unlike Martin, I rather enjoyed the game and chatted with him as we changed into our strips.

"I'm bloody well cheesed off John," groaned Martin, "I'm gonna miss out on football all because o' this crappy game."

I really felt for him because I knew how devoted he was to his beloved sport. But I was glad to be in Bull's team, as I would have only been a spare part sat on the reserve bench for the football team. All the same I found it amusing and couldn't help laughing. "Sorry about that Martin," I mused, "it just struck me as funny. You know why he's done it don't you?"

"Oh aye course I do, we're playing Corporal Gallagher's team and it's a right grudge match ... Bull wants to clobber 'em."

"You've got it in one ... Bull hates losing to him more than any anybody else. You should have seen him t'other week when Gallagher's team trounced us ... he was bloody furious!"

"Yeah I heard about it, but if he thinks I'm gonna get stuck in just to inflate his ego he can get bloody lost!"

Just then the whistle blew for the start of the game. As we lined up Sergeant Bull was standing on the sidelines, but Corporal Gallagher was actually playing in the match as a defender. Only five minutes into the game I collected a ball on the right flank, bounced it past a couple of players and passed it to Martin, who was stood underneath the opposing net with Gallagher facing him. He caught the ball neatly and positioned himself to lob it upwards whilst Gallagher pranced up and down on the spot waving outstretched arms to prevent him from scoring.

Martin grimaced with determination as he drew the ball back to his chest and then to everyone's amazement he very gently threw it at Gallagher's body and then loosely dropped his wrist in a camp manner mouthing with pursed lips, "O-o-oooh!"

191

Everybody on the pitch burst out laughing, but one person on the sidelines didn't see the funny side.

"Gro-o-ogan!" Bull screeched in a frenzied state waving a wooden baton. "Get your bloody arse over here now at the double!"

Martin traipsed off the pitch only to be frogmarched to the guardroom where he was charged with the ridiculous offence of being idle at basketball for which he received the aforesaid jankers.

Poor Martin, he begrudged every minute of his sentence but at least something good came of it .... as he never had to play another game of basketball. I, on the other hand, became a regular choice and took pleasure in it.

Another game I really enjoyed playing was table tennis and I was chosen to be a team player along with two other lads. As it happened some European businessmen threw down the gauntlet, challenging us to play their best three men. We took up the challenge and it turned out to be a really good match. During the contest we set up the table in the NAAFI and each one of us played the opposing three players. We were evenly matched and the outcome was settled in the last game, which I lost 21-17 making the score 5-4 for the entrepreneurs.

"That was one hell of a bout," said the opposing captain, "we must have a return match at our clubhouse."

We did too and it was great. Unlike our sweatshop they had superb facilities, and the table was set up in a large hall with all the mod cons ...a fitness room, showers, air conditioning, the lot! On their home ground we reversed the score 5-4 in our favour. Once again the score was 4-4 but this time I won the last game, gaining revenge on my opponent. To finish off the night we drank some ice cool beer in style by the side of the swimming pool, which they said we were welcome to use during our off duty periods.

I enjoyed the game but the topic in which I excelled was physical training. Along with Pete and some infantry lads we set up a wooden vaulting horse and other apparatus in the open air. As a schoolboy at senior school, PT was always my favourite subject; handstands, back flips, cartwheels ... I revelled in them all. I was very agile and had a natural ability for the sport. I could easily run and spring over the vaulting horse, go into a dive and then do a back flip from the end of the box, landing on my feet. Lots of lads became interested as I walked on my hands and did a lot of other party tricks, and they asked if I would train them. Before long it became a regular exercise and even some of the native workers asked if they could participate. My group of students built up as some Kumba locals, who didn't work on the camp, joined the class. It suited me perfectly, and helped me to relax ... as well as keeping me fit and trim I also made a lot of friends.

My fame spread beyond the camp gates, and one day I was approached by an official from Kumba Town Council, who asked if I would consider taking a job in the Cameroons once I'd finished my stint in Her Majesty's Forces. At the time I still had six months to serve so I didn't take the proposition too seriously. Since then I've often regretted not taking them up on the offer ... who knows what might have come of it.

****

I'll never forget one night when I went out for a quiet drink with Pete. It all started innocently as we sat in one of the bars chatting to the locals.

"Hello Mr John, hello Mr Pete," came a voice from behind us, "I no see you in this bar before."

On turning I saw Dominic. "Hiya Dominic!" I greeted him. "I didn't know you came in here ... you live on the other side of the river in the French Cameroons don't you?"

"That right Mr John, but sometimes I come here to see my cousin Alberto ... he own this bar."

"Good," laughed Pete, "then maybe we can have a drink on the house."

"Drink on house?" queried Dominic still not familiar with our expressions. "I no understand. Why drink on house ... we drink in bar?"

"Yeah," laughed Pete with tongue in cheek, "of course you're right, I like it ... very funny."

Dominic wasn't too sure what Pete was laughing at but joined in all the same, "Yes, it is very funny Mr Pete ... very funny."

Pete knew Dominic hadn't got the joke, making him laugh all the more.

"Where do you usually go for a drink then Dominic?" I asked after the laughter had died down.

"Always Mr John, I take drink in bar near my home across the river … it is much bigger than this one."

Pete's ears pricked up asking, "How have you got here then Dominic?"

"I come here in Jeep of my father."

"Oh aye … is there any chance o' taking us to this bar then?"

"Whoa hang on a minute Pete!" I cut in. "The bar he's talking about is on the French side … it's out of bounds."

"So what; come on John … get cool for once in your life," grinned Pete, who then turned to the young African. "You'll take us and fetch us back won't you Dominic?"

"Yes, if you like I take you and bring you back … but I no want trouble for you."

"Oh never mind about that," Pete laughed, "I'm willing to take the risk if you are John.

"Aye I suppose so," I replied, once again giving way to temptation.

Pete, impatient and raring to go, downed his drink in one, and made his way to the door. "Come on John," he shouted eagerly, "let's get going … we may not get another chance."

"Righto, I'm coming … I'm coming!"

"Good, about time … for a minute I thought you were going to back out."

"Yeah, I would do if I'd any sense."

"Well you haven't. Anyway we're only young once … let's go for it!"

I went for it alright but what I saw when I got outside should have put me off. "What the bloomin' 'eck's that?" I asked Dominic as he started to climb into an old decorated truck that looked like a Gypsy caravan. "I thought you said you'd driven here in a Jeep."

It turned out to be an old Mammi wagon, which had been converted into a bus.

"It is bus of my father … you like?"

"It's a bit dilapidated in't it … are you sure it'll get us there?"

"What you mean Mr John … I no understand?"

"Take no notice of him Dominic," Pete butted in, "if it gets us over the river that'll do me."

"Hey, what about the border patrol policing the bridge?" I asked edgily.

"We'll just have to lie on the floor," quipped Pete quite unconcerned.

"I don't know so much, we'll never get away with it. And don't forget we've to get back across the bridge as well."

"Oh come on John, lighten up a bit, don't be such a killjoy … we'll have a great time."

"Aye alright," I relented climbing into the back of the rickety vehicle, "but I've got a gut feeling I'm gonna regret this."

As we drove towards the bridge I felt agitated at the thought of being discovered by the Regimental Police, yet excited at the prospect of doing something I shouldn't.

"Halt … who goes there!" rapped one of the guards, ordering Dominic to stop. Pete and I lay deadly quiet hidden underneath one of the sagging seats, not daring to move a muscle.

"Hello, 'tis only me," replied Dominic in his chirpy fashion, "I cross river now back to my house."

"Oh it's you Dominic," said the MP, instantly recognising him. "Have you had a good night?"

"Yes Mr Policeman, plenty good … I take plenty beer with soldiers."

"I'll bet you did, and what about the ladies … you have plenty jig a jig as well."

Dominic played along with the conversation, laughing and joking … thankfully, the picket never looked inside the vehicle.

"Bye bye," said Dominic keeping his calm, "I see you again."

"Bloody hell, that was nerve racking," spluttered Pete once we were inside French territory.

"You're not bloody kidding," I replied, "I only hope it's gonna be worth the trouble once we get there."

Almost immediately Dominic left the road and drove for about twenty minutes over a beaten track. Shortly we arrived at a little hamlet in the thick of the jungle.

"There," said Dominic pointing to a large shanty type building, "that is bar that I tell you … it is big no?"

"Oh what a good do," laughed Pete, "let's get in there, I can't wait!"

195

As we entered the French bar it was far bigger than the one back in Kumba with background music playing. I felt rather strange at first as a few locals weighed us up, but settled down when two workers from our camp acknowledged us. Time passed quickly as Pete and I were thoroughly enjoying ourselves, laughing and joking with the friendly natives. But things were about to change. I'd just finished my second drink when one of the camp workers approached us.

"You like jig a jig ... I find you very nice ladies, you have plenty good time?"

"No, it's all right," I answered politely, "but thanks all the same."

"Hey you speak for yourself!" quipped Pete. "I wouldn't mind a jig a jig, I'm feeling rampant ... I haven't had a woman since we left England."

"Come off it Pete," I protested, "we could be in enough trouble as it is already ... let it be!"

My protest fell on deaf ears. Pete ignored me and questioned the man further making it plain that he was raring to go.

"Right Mr Pete you come with me, I take you to hut of very sexy lady ... you have plenty jig a jig."

Pete eagerly followed the man and, to my dismay, Dominic got up as well.

"Where are you going Dominic?" I asked anxiously.

"I go with Mr Pete to make sure he all right."

"Just hang on a minute, I'm not stopping here on my own, I haven't a clue where I am."

I followed the three of them very cautiously aware of danger, and frightened of the unknown. Dominic, sensing my apprehension, assured me there was no need for concern. "Everything will be all right Mr John ... I just no want Mr Pete to lose way."

"I hope so please God, I hope so!" I prayed inwardly.

After walking through thick undergrowth we stopped outside a mud hut with a straw roof amongst a cluster of others like it. "You come with me," said the man addressing Pete.

"Bloody hell, what am I doing here," I panicked as Pete disappeared into a scantily clad hut. Then to make matters worse, when I turned round Dominic wasn't there ... I couldn't believe what

196

was happening. "Oh no," I spluttered to myself, "it can't be ... please don't say that Dominic's deserted me!" By now my nerves were on edge and I was trembling from head to toe as lots of nightmarish thoughts ran through my mind. It was the unknown factor and not knowing what to do that frightened me. But thank goodness my fears were unfounded, as a moment later I heard Dominic's voice.

"All right Mr John, I'm with you now."

"You're with me now, where the flamin' 'eck have you been ... you terrified the living daylights out of me?"

"I sorry Mr John, now you come with me."

"Hang on a minute Dominic ... where are you taking me?"

"It be alright I take you to see nice people."

"Aye alright Dominic," I replied through chattering teeth, "I trust you." I felt that I had no option as he took me to one of the other shanties.

As we entered the hut I found myself in a single candlelit room divided by flimsy cotton curtains. A man and his wife were sat around a small round table alongside a young girl. She was about seventeen and the prettiest thing I'd seen since arriving in Africa. When I looked at her she gave me a sweet alluring smile and bowed her head. The couple offered me a drink and, despite feeling uneasy and out of place, I sat down amongst them.

"Hello Mr John," said the man, "me and wife very happy to meet you."

"And I'm pleased to meet you too," I mumbled.

"This our daughter," said the wife, "her name is Sabia ... she very pretty."

"Yes she is," I replied politely, wondering what was going on.

As the conversation progressed I kept glancing at Sabia and she kept glancing back. I liked the look of her but under the circumstances I didn't know what to do. Then providence took a hand; the young girl slid her hand across the table, placing hers in mine. It felt nice and soft but I couldn't help but feel uncomfortable, as her parents' eyes bore down on me.

"It is all right Mr John," said the lady, "Dominic tell us you good man and our daughter ... she like you."

"Oh thank you very much," I spluttered, still unsure what to do next.

"You come with me Mr John," said Sabia standing up, "we go sit alone." She then drew back one of the flimsy curtains revealing a bed and enticed me towards her. I couldn't believe what was happening and still felt very awkward.

This time the man pointed to the bed nodding, "It is all right Mr John, you go in private place with daughter ... she like you very much."

I went behind the curtain more out of respect and bewilderment than anything else and just sat on the edge of the bed twiddling my thumbs like a stuffed dummy, petrified. I could feel my shoes tapping the floor as my legs shook uncontrollably.

The young girl closed the curtain and sat down at my side, once again taking my hand. I liked the feel of her tender touch but the uneasiness continued and I was simply frozen to the spot.

"You no like me Mr John?" she asked looking at me with sad puppy like eyes.

Her words put me in mind of the scene from the film *South Pacific*. John Kerr, a young naval officer falls in love at first sight with a beautiful Polynesian girl and during a loving embrace she looks at him with the most appealing deep brown eyes; whereupon he takes her into his arms and starts to sing the delightful love song ... *Younger Than Springtime.* But I'm afraid that in my case, romance was not to be.

My thoughts were interrupted as the young girl once again asked, "You no like me Mr John ... I good girl, I make you good wife." Her eyes, despite being sad, were sparkling and vibrant.

"Yes of course I like you Sabia but ......!"

I didn't finish my sentence, as a great deal of commotion erupted outside the hut and I could hear men shouting loudly in an aggressive manner. Suddenly three natives came bursting into the room and one of them was wielding a machete. Luckily for me, the two workers came onto the scene and intervened, striving to calm the situation down. But the man holding the offensive weapon couldn't be reasoned with and he screeched frenziedly.

"I kill white man who take my woman ... I kill ... I kill!"

The next thing I knew, Pete was in the hut, challenging the man to a fight.

"Don't be crazy Pete," I shouted across the room, "use your loaf for crying out loud, we're in the middle of nowhere … if you start something here we'll be slaughtered!"

Thankfully, it dawned on him what I was saying and, realising the gravity of the situation, he took heed. "Bloody hell John you're not wrong … let's get the hell out of here quick!"

We scarpered as fast as we could, hopefully heading back towards the border. It was a dark night but luckily we hit the dirt road and ran with a few screaming natives in hot pursuit. It was horrible … I was actually living my worst nightmare, as I knew that at least one of the natives had a machete. After running blindly for about half a mile we heard friendly honking from a jeep … thank goodness it was Dominic.

"Good lad Dominic," I panted as he pulled up besides us, "get us outa here as quick as you can!"

"I sorry Mr John, Mr Pete, for causing you to have trouble."

"Don't worry about that now," grunted Pete, "like John said … just get going for crying out loud!"

"Phew, that was a close call," I sighed with relief as we left our pursuers behind.

"Aye you're right there," puffed Pete, "we'd have been dead meat if they'd have caught us, they would have cut us to ribbons."

"Yeah, especially the one with the machete … he wasn't in the mood for messing about."

"We're not out of the woods yet John; we've still got to get past the border patrol … if they spot us we're up the creek."

"Tell me something I don't know, it's your bloody fault that we were there in the first place. Anyroad, I couldn't care less anymore … even if they do spot us, that's now't compared to what could have happened back there."

"We'll cross that bridge when we come to it," smirked Pete trying to play down the situation.

"Ha ha, very funny … is that supposed to be a joke? Anyroad, we'll soon find out … I can see it now in the distance."

As we approached the river Pete and I had once again to crouch down under the seats. Thankfully luck was on our side. The guards had changed over and the vigilantes, who didn't suspect a thing, let Dominic pass through the barrier without any fuss. Pete and I sighed with relief as the bus drove off, knowing we'd got off lightly.

"Blimey Pete," I sighed, "we got away with murder there didn't we?"

"Oh I don't know so much," he grinned, "you could actually say we got away with not being murdered."

"Very good, I like it ... you're on form tonight Pete."

We laughed as we passed the Kumba bar where our little escapade had begun and we were both highly delighted to see the camp gates.

"Oh what a beautiful sight," I said, "I never thought I'd be happy to see them Pete."

"I know what you mean John ... they're a sight to behold."

As we passed through the camp barrier one of our mates shouted from the guardroom, "How's it going lads ... have you had another boring night out in the backwoods?"

"Yeah we have," I laughed, "just another humdrum night like any other."

"Little do they know," Pete laughed as we made our way to our hut.

"Aye, you're right there ... tell 'em nowt. Anyway, after all that rumpus I can't wait to hit the sack in peace and quiet."

"No, neither can I," Pete laughed. "That was some night out wasn't it?"

"You can say that again." I said stumbling onto my bed.

I never ventured out of bounds again as it didn't hold the same fascination for me anymore, but every time I crossed over the bridge whilst on official business it brought back memories of that night and of course ... the young girl, Sabia.

****

It was Christmas before we knew it and we decorated the hut with tinsel and Christmas cards from back home. The army very generously supplied us with small regimental Christmas cards with a map of the British Cameroons inscribed on the inside cover. The map showed Victoria, where the *Devonshire* anchored up, and plainly displayed the camps, Buea, Kumba, Bamenda and the Mamfe

200

Airforce Base. I liked the card so much that I sent one home to my mum.

Some soldiers formed an entertainment committee and staged a few shows and a pantomime in the NAAFI, whilst the army put on films in the open air. The feeling of watching a film under the stars was fantastic. It created a good atmosphere, and boosted everyone's morale. I especially enjoyed the first film which, under the circumstances, was very appropriate ... *The League of Gentlemen*, starring Jack Hawkins. It was about a high-ranking army officer who was very disgruntled about the way the army had retired him. He conjured up a plan to rob a bank by using the expertise of other retired soldiers, all highly skilled in their different departments. His plan was flawless, and the way he conned the army and relieved them of some arms and ammunition had every one of us in raptures. Despite perfect planning, the plot failed, but all the same I enjoyed it.

Christmas dinner was different because the commissioned officers waited on the tables; this was a long standing tradition passed down from generation to generation. There were no party hats or Christmas crackers but we still had a laugh; it was relaxing because most of the troops were off duty. Some lads were unlucky enough to be on fatigue duty but even they only had to do a couple of hours. After eating to the point of near bursting I felt guilty, thinking of the poor little blighters outside the camp who might not have anything to eat at all. So without giving it a second thought I obtained a cardboard box and filled it to the brim with loads of bread, potatoes and some turkey leftovers. Sure enough, there they were waiting for their little treats. It made my day to see big smiling beams on their little faces; you'd have thought they'd just won a thousand pounds. I got so carried away that I forgot to watch my back, and to my cost I got caught by one of the MPs.

"Soldier, what d'you think you're playing at!" he roared.

"Oh no, I'm up for the high jump if he charges me," I thought, "surely he could let it go for once ... it's Christmas Day."

He must have read my thoughts, or maybe he'd had a good present from back home, then again he might have even felt sorry for the little blighters; I don't know. What I do know is he seemed to lament and, after reading me the riot act, he let me off with a caution.

That night it was like payday in the NAAFI as we all celebrated to the sound of musical love songs and downed a few cans. The camaraderie amongst the men was fantastic, taking into account that most of them had never set eyes on each other only a year before.

Every soldier missed home and always looked forward to mail from England and this was especially so at this festive time of the year. Some of the lads received treats from home but they gladly shared them amongst all the men. Everybody laughed merrily as they exchanged happenings from back home and showed photographs of their wives, children and sweethearts. It was very stirring to see these tough young men reading their letters with tears rolling down their cheeks. There's no doubt that letters meant so much to everyone in the camp and they were a real boost to the men's morale. That is of course, if it was a love note, and not a dreaded 'Dear John Letter'. Not many lads received a DJL but when one did, he would be completely devastated and there'd be no consoling him. Luckily, no one received one over the Christmas period.

We celebrated Christmas well, but New Year's Eve left an everlasting mark on my memory. My nursing colleagues and I decided to put on a party for the troops, using the clinical room and part of the hospital ward. We worked in league with the Catering Corps and each one of us had a simple task to perform. The infantry soon got wind of the party and some offered to help. My job, along with Jock Hulston from Sterling in Scotland, was making up various sandwiches. He was a driver in the Service Corps and it soon became apparent that he was a character. He'd brought a bottle of scotch and from the start he took a brisk drink and offered me a tot of the amber liquid.

"Cheers mun," he said raising his hands in the air prior to downing his drink in one.

Wanting to be sociable I did the same, whereas he immediately refilled my glass.

"Whoa!" I said knowing full well this was going to be a long night.

"Dunno be so daft, get it down your throoat … it'll do yee the world o' good."

"But I …"

"No boots mun, tonite is New Year's Eve ... the best nite o' the year."

He was very persuasive and anyway I enjoyed the burning sensation at the back of my throat.

"Right Jock you're on ... cheers!"

By the time we'd finished the sandwiches I felt tipsy and the night was still young. Every soldier had contributed something and there was a mountainous pile of beer cans stacked on a table.

One of the lads obtained a record player along with some fifties records from the officers' mess and soon the room was vibrating to the sound of music. By ten o'clock the hospital took on a new light, echoing to the sound of laughter from the boisterous soldiers. Two hours later Maurice collapsed onto the floor due to the effects of alcohol. Along with three other lads we each took a limb, carried him back to our hut and then tucked him in underneath his mosquito net. On this occasion we decided it was wiser not to put another lizard in bed alongside him.

"Trust Maurice to be the first to flake out," laughed Pete.

"I can't understand it Pete," I said, "I've had a lot more to drink than him and I'm all right."

"Aye maybe John but think on, this is the first time Maurice's ever had a drink ... at least to my knowledge."

As the night went on I got merrier and merrier enjoying the festivities along with the troops and as the effects of the alcohol took over I got rid of all my inhibitions. Consequently I got carried away and did something that could have landed me in serious trouble. Captain Smith, along with some English businessmen, decided to join the party and to our surprise the civilians brought their absolutely gorgeous wives with them. I couldn't take my eyes off one of them as she danced around the floor in high heels and silk stockings, displaying the most beautiful pair of legs. I hadn't seen a white woman since leaving the *Devonshire* and I didn't like the QUARANCS anyway because of their pretentious ways. But this ravishing lady was desirable, and her very presence made my mouth water triggering off my hormones, especially when she danced by me sending off a whiff of perfume. The music changed to a smoochy number and my pulse started to race as my heart pounded faster and faster. As the couple passed by I got a strong impulse and just couldn't stop myself ... without thinking I tapped the bloke on the shoulder.

"Excuse me please," I said taking hold of the lady's arm. She appeared a little surprised at first but responded in a pleasant manner, making me feel completely at ease. As I stared into her deep blue eyes she gave me a pert smile, endearing me to her all the more ... I was completely smitten.

"And what's your name soldier boy?" she asked politely.

"John," I smiled back.

"Oh what a gorgeous smile you have and such beautiful teeth," she murmured softly, boosting my ego.

"And you're a beautiful lady," I answered drawing her close to me.

She responded by caressing my shoulders with her hands and before I knew it I was tenderly kissing her neck. Whether her husband was neglecting her I don't know ... what I do know is she enjoyed the attention and responded by kissing my cheek. As I danced by some soldiers they expressed their delight.

"Yeah, go on John ... give her a kiss for me!"

I didn't need any encouragement ... this was one 'eck of a lady and I readily grasped the moment. I was totally besotted and didn't notice the resentful look on the civilians' faces and to tell the truth, at the time I didn't give a damn.

My moment of bliss came to an end as Captain Smith tapped me on the shoulder.

"Excuse me soldier," he snarled. Glaring at me, he added, "Report to my office at 14-00hours tomorrow!"

"Please yourself," I thought, "I haven't broken any rules." Turning to the lady I smiled, "Thank you ma'am, that was delightful ... Happy New Year!"

"And the same to you John," she smiled back, "take care."

"By 'eck that was nice," I murmured as I walked off the floor to be greeted by some infantry lads.

"I'll bet you enjoyed that you lucky swine," they all laughed giving me the nod.

"I did that lads, I think I'm in love ... she's absolutely stunning."

Just then Bill rang a bell, temporarily bringing the festivities to a halt. "Attention everybody it's countdown time, get ready ... 5 – 4 – 3 – 2 - 1 ... Happy New Year!"

Everyone spontaneously began to sing *Auld Lang Syne* and during the celebrations I made my way towards the gorgeous lady to offer her my best wishes and a New Year's kiss. But there was no chance ... the officer barred my path and warned me off. "On your way Private Cowell, don't push it ... you're in enough trouble as it is!"

"Bullshit ... up yours!" I thought. I didn't get a kiss, as the businessmen grouped together cordoning her off but they couldn't stop me from silently mouthing through pursed lips, "Happy New Year!"

She nodded back in acknowledgement and blew me a kiss across the palm of her upturned hand, annoying the civilians even more.

My elation was interrupted as another soldier flopped to the floor in a drunken state. I couldn't believe it ... this time it was Pete and he was out cold.

"Bloomin' 'eck Bill, who'd o' thought it," I blurted, "Pete can really take his ale; it's not like him to flake out."

"I know that," laughed Bill, "but he's been on the ale since four o'clock ... he's fairly knocked some cans back."

"Aye, so have I, but I feel all right," I smirked

Just like we did with Maurice, four of us grabbed a leg and carted him back to the hut. As I tucked in the mosquito net I was convinced Pete was having us on. When we got back to the clinical room the celebrations were still in full swing but sadly, the lady of my dreams had gone along with the captain and company.

Spud Murphy, in his own brand of humour, started to poke fun at me, "Get some ale into your belly John," he scoffed, "cos it's gonna be your last chance for a long while."

"What are you talking about, I haven't done anything wrong."

"You don't think so do you not? All I can say is I wouldn't like to be in your shoes."

"How come?"

"How come," he smirked gulping down another beer, "come off it, you know what a bastard that captain is ... if he has his way they'll lock you up and throw away the key."

"How can they do that, I haven't broken any army rules?"

"Army rules my arse, I've been in the army twenty years and I can tell you now it doesn't pay to get on the wrong side of a captain, especially one like him who's pushing for promotion."

"Blimey," I said getting worried, "did I go that far?"

"Did you go that far ...you should o' seen the look on his face when you were kissing that woman? As far as he is concerned, you've undermined his authority and showed him up in front of his friends ... he was bloody frothing at the mouth."

"Oh bloomin' 'eck!" I moaned, "I didn't mean to do owt wrong, I was just having a good time and got carried away."

"Bloody hell!" roared Murphy breaking out into a fit of laughter. "Just look at your gloomy face, I'm only joking. Mind you, I still think he'll pull you over the coals and maybe give you a few days' jankers but that's about it. Anyway, Happy New Year! Get some more ale down you."

"Aye you're right Spud ... I haven't done anything serious have I?"

"Ha ha ha!" roared a few lads all at once. "Not bloody much you haven't."

"Not to worry John," said one of them, handing me a can of beer, "get this in your belly and stuff 'em all."

"Cheers," I retaliated, "Happy New Year!"

I don't remember a thing after that, as everything started to go hazy. My next recollection was waking up the following morning underneath my mosquito net with the most horrendous hangover in the world. Just like the others before me, I'd actually been carted back to my bed in a collapsed state. I couldn't lift my head off the pillow and the slightest movement made me feel like spewing my guts up. I gradually managed to dangle my legs over the side of the bed and Spud Murphy was staring at me with a can of beer in each hand.

"Here John, have a swig o' this," he laughed, "the hair of the dog an' all that."

"Ur-r-ggh!" I retched. "Take it away ...it smells awful!"

'E-eh, just look at you," he scoffed unsympathetically, "and you were only mocking the others last night cos they flaked out."

I'd no answer to that and just bent over clasping my head in my hands, feeling sorry for myself. I tried lying down to sleep it off but no chance … the room started to spin as all the contents of my stomach churned over, making a gurgling sound.

"O-o-hh, somebody please stop this roundabout and let me get off!"

It's a good job I wasn't on duty that day; I felt like I was dying … I'd had a hangover before but nothing like this. Maurice and Pete were still sleeping but the rest of the lads were in high spirits laughing and joking. I could hear loud music and every beat pounded 'boom boom boom' making my temples throb. I just had to get out of the hut into the fresh air, but as soon as I took a deep breath my stomach muscles tightened and went into spasm, causing me to retch. No matter what I did I couldn't get any respite from that abysmal feeling and for the first time in my life I couldn't eat.

To make matters worse the captain sent word, summoning me to his office. At this point I hadn't been officially charged but I made my way to see him full of foreboding.

"Blast it!" I mumbled, "I thought he might have let it go … what with it being New Year's Day an' all."

Even though I didn't feel in a fit state to argue my case I was determined to say my piece, and canny enough to address him in the manner befitting an officer.

"Right Private Cowell, what have you got to say for yourself about what happened last night?" he rapped as I stood to attention.

"I beg your pardon Sir but I'm not quite sure what you mean," I replied acting naively.

"You what!" he roared. "Don't get clever with me soldier or I'll have you thrown in the brig! The way you acted with my friend's wife was appalling."

"I'm sorry Sir but I don't think the lady or I did anything wrong."

"Damn you man … she didn't do anything wrong but it's not her I'm on about … it's you!"

He'd taken the bait … this was the very thing I wanted him to say and the very manner I wanted him to say it in. He hadn't followed the army code and so, in my mind, his aggressive manner now gave me the right to talk to him on level terms … man to man.

"Quoting your own words … she didn't do anything wrong, which means that I didn't do anything wrong either."

"For crying out loud Private Cowell," he said regaining a little composure, "she was a guest of mine and you showed me up in company."

"With all due respects Sir my friends and I worked very hard organising that party for the troops. You took it on your own head to invite civilians, which indirectly makes you responsible. All I can say in my defence is that it was New Year's Eve and I was thoroughly enjoying myself. I'd drunk loads of beer with the lads and I can't deny that I was very attracted to the lady. But I must add that we didn't do anything behind closed doors … it was all in the open."

At that I detected a slight snigger at the corner of his mouth but he suppressed it. Deep down I suspected that he was more embarrassed than angry.

He pondered for a while before saying, "Go on, get out of my sight and don't let it happen again … especially in front of me!"

As I made my way back to the hut I took a big breath of fresh air and chuckled, "Ah well John lad, all's well that ends well … Happy New Year!"

I was relieved at the outcome but was still suffering badly with a terrible hangover. I felt like taking myself off to bed but it was Sunday and I was determined to start the New Year off by attending the afternoon church service over the river. Jock Hulston, my Scottish boozing partner from the night before, offered to run me there in one of the Landrovers and we got there in ample time. The church was packed to the doors with standing room only and the congregation sang so beautifully with a rhythm that only African people have. On this occasion, Jock was in no hurry to get back to camp which gave me ample opportunity to speak with the missionaries, and this was when I bought the Sunday Roman Missal, which all the dear ladies signed for me. The local priest also stamped it with the official hallmark of Kumba.

****

I enjoyed army routine because it took a lot of stress out of my life. I'd no major decisions to make and I had everything laid on a plate ... all I had to do was follow orders.

I didn't even mind the strict discipline and the pettiness, but one thing I didn't like was injustice; and in my case the army did something unforgivable. Their sin against me was bad, but the way they treated one of the local natives was abysmal.

There was a corporal in the infantry and to say he was a bastard is an understatement ... he was a bully, a barbaric fiend and a beast all wrapped up in one. Like all bullies he was a coward, using intimidating tactics against unsuspecting victims much smaller and weaker than himself. He was a regular soldier in his late twenties and definitely got away with flagrant offences that a National Serviceman would have been locked up for. Being a tall man with a fine physique he weighed around eighteen stones, and was forever getting drunk and throwing his weight around, using bullyboy tactics. Without a doubt he was a despicable ruffian and his reputation preceded him wherever he went. Amongst the troops, his nickname was 'Corporal Bullyboy'.

I happened to be on duty one morning in the clinical room when the medical officer approached me.

"John," he said, "I've got a soldier here who's fallen into a ditch and badly damaged his right hand on some rocks and he's got severe lacerations to three fingers that need suturing. I'm going to start him on penicillin injections so I've told him to attend every day for a jab and a change of dressings."

"Fine Sir, leave it with me," I replied.

Nobody was more surprised than me when Corporal Bullyboy entered the room. When I saw his hand I actually felt sorry for him, but then he started to shoot his mouth off.

At first I made a joke of it, "Bloomin' 'eck! You must have had a skinful last night ... did you fall into the ditch on the way home?"

He just scoffed and laughed arrogantly. "You don't really think I did this on a rock do you?"

"How d'you mean?" I queried. "That's how Doctor Whittaker thinks you did it."

He sniggered again and then started to brag, "Of course that's what the doctor thinks you idiot ... that's what I wanted him to think

… for the record an' all that. I busted my hand on the thick skull of a wog, knocking his teeth out … ye-eah, I really gave it to him!"

"Why, how come," I asked pricking my ears up, "what happened?"

"E-eh, me and mi mates went out on the town last night and got tanked up, and we were still in the local bar knocking 'em back at three o'clock this morning."

"Oh yeah, and did you get into a fight then?" I asked so as to glean more information from him.

"No did we bloody hell but there was a nigger in there flashing his wallet about with loads o' money in it. He was getting right up my nose, so I decided I was gonna have him and his money as well. Mi mates left but I waited outside the bar and hid in some bushes, and when he came out I jumped him and gave him a right teddying."

His vulgar expressions and mannerisms repulsed me and the pity I felt for him earlier completely left me. He was completely devoid of human compassion and revelled in the fact that he had afflicted agony and misery on a fellow human being. He certainly didn't reflect the typical soldier, as most of the troops got on very well with the local natives, working alongside them, both on and off the camp. Despite my repulsion I still had to treat him, but I wanted him to feel some pain, so prior to stitching his fingers I didn't administer any local anaesthetic.

"Ouch that hurts you bastard!" he moaned as I put three sutures into each finger. "Can't you numb 'em first?"

It became apparent that, although he liked to inflict pain on others, he didn't like it when he was on the receiving end.

I came up with an excuse, "There's no point because the process of numbing is more painful than the actual stitching. I would have used Lignocaine if you'd o' needed five or more stitches in each finger."

"Aye all right, but get it over and done with will you for crying out loud!" he squawked.

I lied about the anaesthetic but I didn't care … it was worth it to hear him squeal like a pig.

"Serves you bloody right!" I thought. I then derived pleasure from giving him an injection with the biggest needle I could find.

"Ou-uch … that hurt, you bloody little wimp! What did you use … a flaming darning needle?"

Once again I thought how he got sheer pleasure out of inflicting pain on others but, like all cowards, he didn't like pain himself.

"That's better," he gloated when I'd finished dressing his fingers, "this'll give me and my mates something to laugh about."

"You bloody bastard!" I thought as he strutted haughtily from the treatment room as though he'd done something heroic.

I mentioned what he'd said to the medical officer but his reply was, "You might as well let it go John … it's just his word against yours."

"But surely Sir, it's wrong if he gets away with it scot-free."

"I know that but my hands are tied because I can only report what he told me."

I felt rather dejected as I left the surgery, but that wasn't the end of it. Later that day the camp was in chaos as civilian police visited the camp along with the injured man to voice a complaint.

I saw the poor fellow and he was in a right state with swollen lips, stitches in his nose and puffed up eyes. He was only of slight build and looked like a slip of a boy in comparison to the thug who had attacked him. It was only when the fragile little man talked that I detected some front teeth missing. To my delight, two MPs arrested Bullyboy and marched him off to the guardroom. He was officially charged and a hearing was set up for two days hence, pending a court martial.

"Good," I thought, "he's got his just desserts." I couldn't have been more wrong.

Next morning an infantry sergeant accompanied by the sergeant major came to see me in the clinical room to discuss the incident. It soon became apparent that they were rather power crazy and definitely not men of honour.

"Right medic," the sergeant enquired, "I believe you treated a corporal yesterday who'd busted his hand on some rocks?"

"If you mean that bastard corporal who assaulted that poor little native bloke, then yes I did."

"That'll do soldier, we'll have less of that talk; keep your lip buttoned or you'll be in serious trouble! Anyway, we're here to get certain things sorted out."

211

"Right Sarge, what can I do for you?"

"Sarge!" he snarled clenching his fist. "Who do you think you're talking to you little runt? When you address me soldier, my title is Sergeant and stand to attention when I'm talking to you!"

"Yes Sergeant," I answered, reluctantly obeying his order.

"You can take that look off your face you blown up medic," said the sergeant major taking over the conversation, "or I'll put you on a charge for insubordination." After dressing me down and making it plain that he was in charge he then got down to the real issue. "Right, we've come here to sort out these trumped up charges against one of our corporals. I've read the medical officer's version of events, which coincides exactly with what the accused says in his statement about falling into a ditch and injuring his hand on a rock. He paused for a minute before continuing, "U-um, and seeing as how you treated his injuries we're going to summon you to attend a court hearing as a witness for the defence ... and we want you to say exactly what is written in the doctor's report."

But Sir, the corporal's bound to say that isn't he ... do you want to know what really happened?"

"Quiet Soldier," rapped the sergeant almost frothing at the mouth, "I've told you once already ...we'll have no more loose talk. When you go into that courtroom just repeat exactly what we tell you to say ... understood?"

"Understood perfectly Sergeant," I replied letting them both think I would go along with their hoodwinking tactics.

"Right Private Cowell," growled the sergeant major as they turned to leave, "report to the officers' quarters at 10-00hours tomorrow morning on the dot! And don't mention the case to anyone until after the hearing or I'll have yours guts for garters ... understood!"

"Aye and up yours you corrupt lot!" I sniggered inwardly. "I'll be there all right but you're in for a shock maties ... if you think I'm gonna lie under oath you're one off, get me on the stand and I'm going to tell the truth and nothing else." I actually looked forward to the challenge despite the fact that I would be making enemies of these so-called officers and that they could make life difficult for me. I couldn't wait to see the looks on their faces once they got me in the witness box, especially Bullyboy's.

Next morning, the day of reckoning, I had to attend the hearing in my dress uniform and I couldn't find my cap badge. Pete lent me his but by the time I got to the officers' mess I was two minutes late and all the other witnesses were present.

"Where've you been?" roared the sergeant major. You should have been here at 10-00hours like everybody else."

"Sorry Sir I ….."

"I don't want excuses, just get in line and wait your turn to be called," adding, "and after this hearing you're on a charge."

I was fuming but I didn't protest because there was no point, as he wasn't a man to be reasoned with. I sat around all day with the others waiting to give evidence. One by one they were called into the tribunal before me, whilst I hung about impatiently. Then at four o'clock word came via the court clerk that the case had been adjourned until the following day. I had to attend at 10-00hours again, and this time I was there with time to spare. On the second day all other witnesses were called in, leaving me with butterflies in my stomach, as I practised what I was going to say. I felt very nervous but was determined to stand my ground. Then to my dismay the proceedings were adjourned yet again. On the third day an officer informed me that I would be called upon around 11-00hours.

"Thank goodness for that," I thought, "let's get it over and done with, I don't fancy hanging around all day again." I was mulling over things in my mind when all of a sudden I heard loud cheering from the courtroom.

"Ye-eah, great stuff!" yelled a few of Bullyboy's mates as they came out of the hearing. "Not guilty … he's got off with it!"

I couldn't believe my ears. Bullyboy had violated human rights, viciously beating the poor bloke to within an inch of his life and the army had allowed him to get off scot-free.

I was totally shocked and appalled by the decision and the unfairness of it all … to me it was corruption at its worst. The army hated the stigma attached to a court martial, and after this tribunal it came out of it as pure as driven snow. But in my mind the presiding officers and all concerned had a lot to answer for … Corporal Bullyboy was as guilty as sin and they knew it. They'd set a standard of bad behaviour, allowing him to carry on in his evil, cruel, shameful ways. As he came from the courtroom he stood arrogantly on the step in a victory pose with a sly sneer on his face, and, raising his arm in the air, he clenched his fist.

"What a mockery of justice," I thought, "it's unbelievable that he's gotten away with it." I was fuming but felt helpless, as I knew he couldn't be tried again for the same offence. As he passed by me he nodded and smiled but his smile was like a shadow under a stone, displaying the true character of the man … or should I say the beast. The calibre of the man was that of a snake.

At the time I didn't fully understand all the workings of the law, but with a bit more knowledge I would have reported it to the civil police and maybe the poor bloke could have taken out a civil action against the brute.

The trial was over but I still hadn't been excused. With the result going in the army's favour I thought that the sergeant major might relent and let me off for my little misdemeanour of being two minutes late … there was no chance; I tried protesting but to no avail. He relished the power he held over me and seemed to derive pleasure from it. He ordered me to attention and then frogmarched me in front of the commanding officer.

I mentioned my cap badge, as I couldn't come up with anything else but it was fruitless … the CO was unforgiving and gave me seven days' jankers. I couldn't believe what was happening to me all because of a bombastic bullyboy. I resented the fact that the hooligan was cleared, feeling I was being punished indirectly because of his crime.

"I'm not taking this lying down," I thought, "even if they can't try him again I'm gonna say my piece." But as soon as I mentioned the incident I was shot down in flames.

"That will do soldier, that case is done and dusted," rapped the CO, "and I don't want another word mentioned on the subject or I'll sentence you to seven days in the cells without pay. Do you understand?"

"Perfectly Sir," I replied with an insolent look on my face.

"Take that look off your face soldier or I'll have you for insubordination."

"With all due respect Sir I am not being insubordinate, the look on my face is born of frustration because I feel that my hands are tied." I certainly didn't want throwing in the brig with loss of pay but I couldn't stop myself from adding. "I may not be allowed to talk about this injustice in army circles but I feel it is my duty to report it to the local police." If looks could kill I would have dropped dead on the spot.

The commandant made it quite plain what he thought about my remark, "Just remember one thing Private Cowell ... you're confined to the camp for seven days and if it comes to my notice that you've put one foot outside the camp gates you'll be in serious trouble ... do you understand what I'm saying?"

"Yes Sir!"

He pondered for a while stroking his chin then dismissed me. "Right soldier you can go now, but take heed of what I said."

As I left the room it was obvious that the CO wasn't very happy with me and I had a feeling that I hadn't heard the last of it. It didn't take very long for my premonition to come true ... four days to be exact.

Mark Radiven and I received orders that we were being transferred to Bamenda, another hundred and fifty miles further north, into mountainous terrain.

"It must be a coincidence," I thought, "they wouldn't go out of their way so much ... surely not?" Coincidence or not I had to pack my kitbag and on the last day of my jankers I was heading for my second camp way up in the mountains.

****

CHAPTER SIX

BAMENDA & OUTPOSTS

After bidding farewell to my friends, including the natives, I climbed into a Landrover alongside Mark Radiven and we headed for our new camp. I found it really daunting as we travelled through dense bush country along makeshift roads. We'd over 150 miles to go and I felt every bump and cranny. Besides being muddy there were potholes everywhere and steep cliff drops to one side of the track. Paddy, an Irish man in the Service Corps, who was driving us to Bamenda, had to focus hard on the road; otherwise we could have had a catastrophe. He had a great sense of humour as I found out when I expressed my concern.

"Bloody hell Paddy! I wouldn't like to drive on these roads."

"Just shut your eyes like I do," he laughed.

To make matters worse, every now and then large juggernauts, transporting gigantic logs, would come tearing towards us at great speed without giving way an inch. After travelling for hours on end along dense jungle roads we finally came to open country and after about a mile started to climb steadily up a steep escarpment, which gave way to panoramic views over the surrounding territory. This particular region was known as the Savannah Uplands and Bamenda was situated way up the mountain, giving it a great vantage point. In comparison to the thick jungle surrounding Kumba this region was hilly with deep valleys and gorges covered in bamboo thickets, making it an ideal habitat for terrorists. The outlaws had wreaked havoc for years throughout the country and despite many bombing raids the French couldn't control their activities. It was nigh impossible to track them down, as the bandits, having lived there all their lives, knew every nook and cranny of the area.

However, after the arrival of the British battalion, things took on a different light. The King's Own Borderers, highly trained in jungle warfare and close combat, were led by many highly experienced veterans from the Second World War, who were used to patrolling all types of rugged terrain. Constant patrolling and routine roadblocks became normal routine with only a few incidents.

When I reached the Bamenda camp I immediately noticed a difference in the atmosphere. The air was fresher and smelt cleaner, making it pleasanter and much easier to breathe. Due to the fresher climate I often got the impression that I was back in England on a hot summer's day. But one thing that brought me back to reality was the presence of snakes. I only ever saw one but I was well aware that there were plenty around because there were always plenty of snakeskins lying around the place which the reptiles had shed during their life cycles.

The monsoon season had finished and the hot sun parched the mud so much that it gave off a red dust, covering all the vehicles and equipment. Troops returning to camp after being out on patrol looked like Red Indians.

Unlike Kumba, all billets were tents set up on grass within the confines of a disused racetrack. The cookhouse stood near the outer fringe of the camp and resembled a circus big-top. Mark and I were the only medics amongst forty men, as the remaining nursing orderlies were out on patrol, supporting other troops. We both slept in a tent which housed eight men, along with other attachments. One of these happened to be Neville Atkinson, the old school friend of mine, who I hadn't seen since leaving the *Devonshire*. I knew from back on the ship that Neville was in the Signal Corps, but what I didn't know was that he was the camp's disc jockey. I discovered this on my way to breakfast on Sunday morning when I heard his voice over the Tannoy. I couldn't believe my ears when I heard him congratulating one of the troops on his birthday and, especially for the lad, he put on a record by Neil Sedaka, *Tra la la la, la la la la lah, Happy Birthday Sweet Sixteen.* Neville must have been a keen fan of Neil Sedaka, as the next two songs he played were, *Oh Carol, I am but a fool,* and *Breaking up is hard to do.* I had a good laugh about it with him when I next saw him.

"Bloomin' 'eck Nev," I joked, "you must be the first ever DJ in the Cameroons."

"Aye you never know John," he laughed back, "I might get discovered out here and become a millionaire."

It was good to have Neville around, someone from my own town; I felt I was going to settle down more quickly now into my new surroundings.

It was after chatting with Neville that I made my way to the local Mankon Church, which was situated in the midst of some shanty type huts. Like Kumba, it was served by missionaries and so I took my Roman Catholic Missal along with me and asked them to sign it for me. Just like in Kumba, the priest stamped it with the church's official mark.

****

The hospital was very small in comparison to Kumba, in fact it was more like a treatment room and Mark and I were the only two medics in attendance. Mark had worked as a clerk and so he did all the paperwork, whereas I did most of the nursing duties. This worked out fine for both of us. I treated the men for minor ailments and lacerations, but if a soldier took ill, he was usually confined to bed in his tent and I would pay him regular visits to keep an eye on him and to make sure he got his meals. Confinement to his tent had an advantage over being in hospital, as lads around the camp would help out and encourage the lad; troops returning from patrol would muck in to cheer the patient up.

I'd treated various conditions in Kumba, but in Bamenda I came across different ailments. No one suffered from the dreaded fungal rash, but quite a few suffered from dreadful earache. My heart used to go out to some of the lads because the pain was so severe and constant that they felt like banging their heads against a wall. I felt a bit helpless at times, because all I could do was to give them prescribed analgesics, but nothing seemed to ease the pain and they eventually had to be transferred to Buea, and sometimes from there to the civilian hospital in Tiko. It must have been something to do with the altitude in Bamenda that affected their ears; I don't really know, but I do know that it seemed to settle once they reached the main camp.

One lad got inflammation and swelling of the lower legs, especially his ankles and it looked like elephantitis with blisters. We were quite alarmed, as it looked like leprosy. Another soldier contracted a seriously infected belly button with lots of pus oozing from it, which had been caused by an insect bite or some kind of bug. In both cases all I could do, besides giving painkillers, was to clean the wounds every day and apply dressings. There was no sign of improvement in either patient and, as they were both in obvious distress, they were transferred to Mamfe, an Airforce Base, which had better facilities, and from there to Buea. Once the patients left Bamenda, I didn't usually see them again, but rumour had it that they weren't treated very well at Mamfe. The Airforce boys had a reputation amongst the troops that they looked down on us army personnel and thought we were the scum of the earth. I could never understand the logic in this because when any of the air corps visited our campsite they were always treated well.

****

Just like at my first camp the soldiers employed natives to do their chores for a minimal fee. But unlike Kumba, where we had hut boys, the attendant for our tent was a young native girl called Lucy. She was very good, and like Pius Tashi, did our washing, cleaned our boots and generally kept the place neat and tidy. I got on well with Lucy and we became very good friends ... I liked her and she made it clear that she liked me.

One day whilst hanging out clothes on a washing line she approached me and put her arms around my neck saying, "You marry me Mr John, I go back to England with you ... I promise I make you good wife."

"I like you too Lucy but it wouldn't work ... England is so different to out here in Africa, you wouldn't be happy."

She just smiled, "I be happy anywhere in world with you Mr John."

I felt a bit awkward, as I didn't want to hurt her feelings. "You may think that now Lucy but a few years from now things will look different, you will find a nice man out here and will have many children ... you'll see."

"Alright Mister John," she laughed showing a set of pearly white teeth, "but I always keep you in my prayers and my heart."

"Yes and I'll always keep you in mine," I replied feeling very touched by her manner.

The strong affinity that we had between us was to last throughout my time in Bamenda.

****

Like in Kumba, Bamenda had a small market place, but it was about three quarters of a mile from camp at the lower end of a steep mountain road. Still, I enjoyed the trek, especially now it was the dry season. It was a quaint little bazaar, which sold trinkets and other things, but they mainly dealt in clothes. The items were very cheap and skilled tailors could make suits or anything else to order.

One day whilst I was rummaging through some wares Mark called me over. "Hey John have you seen this material, it'll make a cracking shirt ... it's got all the colours of the rainbow in it."

"Bloomin' 'eck, you're right," I spluttered, "I'd love one made out of that."

"I make you shirt soldier," said the stallholder waving a tape measure keen to make a sale.

"Oh yeah, how much?"

"Only eight shillings ... it very good quality."

"No thank you, I like it but not that much." I answered going into the haggling mode.

"But please, it very good price and I take plenty much trouble to make so it fit you perfect."

"I'll give you four shillings ... not a penny more."

"No no, I no can do ... I have plenty big family to feed. The best I can do be seven shillings"

"Oh yeah, I've heard that one before."

"But I no speak with you before sir ... I no understand."

"It's alright... that's just an expression. I'll tell you what ... I'll give you six shilling, and that's it."

"Right, you give me six shilling now ... I make you shirt."

"Whoa hang on a minute ... I'll give you two shillings now and another four shillings when the shirt is ready."

He shook his head a little then agreed to the deal, "Righto sir, I measure you now, you come next week and shirt be ready."

So the deal was struck, but on the way back to camp Mark was more than a little suspicious. "That might be the last you see of that two bob John ... you're more trusting than me."

"You might be right Mark but somehow I don't think so. Anyway, wait and see." My gut feeling about the gentleman was right. When I went back the following week my shirt was hung on a hanger waiting to be collected.

The man called me over as soon as he saw me, "You try on shirt soldier man... I think you like." I didn't just like it; I loved it ... it fit like a glove. I felt like I was in Hawaii. I wore it that night and strutted about the NAAFI like a peacock. I liked it so much that I ordered a couple more to take home as presents for my two brothers.

This got me to thinking that I should also get something for my three sisters. I glanced at another stall and saw an array of underslips and bodices with flower like buttons down the front. It put me in mind of a small milliner's shop back home, which stood facing the entrance to the Market Hall. I remember my twin sister Mary used to frequent the shop, especially on Saturdays, as did other young girls. There were some nice oddments on the stall and so once more I went into the haggling mode.

Over the next few weeks I bought more souvenirs for my friends back home and an extra special one for my mum. The friendly haggling continued and my healthy relationship with the locals continued to grow.

****

The routine was much different to Kumba, and although I was stationed in the main camp I spent most of my time working in small outposts situated about twenty miles from Bamenda close to the French border. The three prominent outstations were at Sante Coffee, a disused coffee plantation, Sante Customs and Pinyin. My first taste of this different type of patrolling was at Sante Customs, so called because it housed the Customs and Excise building, which was guarded by Nigerian officials and French policemen. The radio operator detailed to the assignment happened to be Neville. The only road through the small hamlet had to pass through a barrier similar to a level crossing back home, and this was raised and lowered as every vehicle passed through. Every mode of transport, be it an army truck or a civilian horse and cart, was thoroughly vetted before being

221

allowed to pass through to the French Cameroons. Prior to our coming to the Cameroons the surrounding area had, for years, been an ideal hideaway for terrorists. Due to the experience of our veteran soldiers and the hard work of the troops, things were now very different.

The Platoon that I was attached to had set up camp establishing tents amidst some old farmyard buildings close to the Customs and Excise building. The tents were much smaller than the ones back in the main camp at Bamenda and accommodated just two men. But I had a special tent all to myself, which stored all the medical supplies. I thoroughly enjoyed working in this small field hospital because I had lots of responsibility and, in many ways, was my own boss. I was in my element and felt as though I'd slotted right into my niche.

During my posting in Plymouth I'd learnt to drive and now my driving licence held me in good stead. At this small outpost I had a vehicle at my disposal, a covered jeep which had been adapted for use as a miniature ambulance. It was fitted out with a canvas bed, splints and small units, containing First Aid supplies and other equipment. A tent had been erected with limited medical supplies, specially set up so soldiers could attend sick parade. There was no doctor around, so I was totally accountable for the health and safety of this small platoon of soldiers. It worked on the principle that I assessed soldiers' complaints myself, and if I thought it necessary I could excuse them from certain duties. If a soldier became seriously ill I got in touch, via Neville, with the main camp back in Bamenda. If necessary I transported the patient back to the main hospital to be seen by the medical officer.

Every morning during inspection parade, I routinely gave each soldier a Paludrin tablet and then attended to sick parade. On one occasion a soldier named Dave came to the tent.

"Yes Dave," I said, "what can I do for you?"

"Well I'm supposed to go out on a route march today with Sergeant Jones' mob and my feet are bloomin' killing me."

"Right then, take your boots off and let's have a look." After assessing him I said, "I can see what your trouble is, you've got some small blisters forming just near your big toes."

"So, what does that mean then?"

"It means that you won't have to go on the route march after all 'cos I'm excusing you from wearing boots for a couple of days."

"Great!" he yelled, "that'll do me."

"Here," I said handing him a slip of paper, "give this sick note to your sergeant and you shouldn't have any problems."

He didn't have any, but I did.

I was attending to another lad when the sergeant came bursting into the tent and he was fuming. "What the bloody hell do you think you're doing Cowell excusing one of my squad from wearing boots?"

"His feet are badly blistered Sarge," I replied, "he needs to rest his feet for a couple of days or they'll get a lot worse."

"I don't bloody well care what his feet are like; he's going out with the rest of the squad and that's it!"

"But Sergeant he can't go, if he does ….."

"Shut your mouth medic; he's going and that's bloody final!"

Not to be put off I answered arrogantly, "OK … then on your own head be it."

"You what soldier," he fumed, "who the bloody hell do you think you are? You're not a doctor, just a bloody jumped up medic!"

"All right Sergeant, if that's the way you see it you make him march; but I have to remind you that the medical officer has authorised me to use my own discretion in cases like this. If you still choose to send Dave out on a route march I'll have to make out a report to that effect."

"You slimy little weasel," he scoffed frothing at the mouth, "don't come the wise guy with me or you'll wish you'd never been born."

"I'm not coming the wise guy Sergeant; I'm just trying to do my duty like I've been trained to do."

"Right Private Cowell," he stammered as he turned to leave the tent, "you've won this round, but let's see if you win the next one, eh?"

"Oh crikey!" I thought as he stormed out, "I hope I haven't made an enemy of the sergeant; that's all I need."

Unfortunately I had and it didn't take long before he wreaked his revenge. I was looking at the listed orders the following day and noticed that he had placed me on guard duty that night. He was out of order because all medics were exempt from doing guard and he knew it.

I approached him about it but he wouldn't listen and just started bellowing. "Get away from me you little creep, you'll do guard duty and like it!"

I could see he was in no mood to be reasoned with so I had no option but to carry out his will. I remember it well because it was actually my twenty-second birthday. Not to be beaten, I was determined to do something about it despite the consequences; I wasn't keen on reporting him but he'd left me with no choice.

"Sod it!" I thought, "he's not getting away with it … if I don't mention it, he'll have me on guard duty for ever and a day."

My superior was furious and made it clear to the sergeant that it mustn't happen again under any circumstances. The NCO didn't take kindly to being reprimanded and made things difficult for me in other areas. But, thankfully, something happened to alter things. It really put all my expertise to the test.

Smithy, a regular soldier in his platoon, had a nasty accident in the foothills just outside our little station and sustained a complicated fracture of his tibia, one of the long bones in the lower half of the leg. The broken bone had pierced the skin and cut through a main artery. I was on the spot within minutes and the man was in a bad way. He'd lost a lot of blood and was lying on the ground in a state of shock and his breathing was laboured.

"Come on John lad," I panicked inwardly, "you'll have to muster up all your experience for this one." My mind raced back to Queen Elizabeth Barracks in Crookham where I had undergone sixteen weeks of arduous training in readiness for this kind of incident. One thing that all the tutors drummed into us during the strict regime was the importance of First Aid. They pointed out that the first person on the scene of any accident was the most vital, and made it clear that whatever was done at that point could be a lifesaver. I remembered well them stressing that it's no good getting a man to hospital with a broken arm or anything else if he's died of asphyxiation or bled to death before you get him there.

"We haven't moved him medic," said the sergeant bringing me back to reality, "we didn't want to make things worse."

"Right Sergeant, I can see your mode of thinking," I said after checking the bloke's airway for signs of obstruction, "but we're going to have to get him sat up."

"Why's that … wouldn't it be better to leave him lying there until you've stabilised his leg? And anyway what about the wound … he's bleeding like a stuffed pig."

"I understand your concern Sergeant, but it's imperative that I make sure his air passages are clear so he can breathe properly. I'm aware of the bleeding and I'll attend to it as soon as we have him propped up"

"Aye righto medic, you're in charge," he said whilst assisting me to move the soldier.

"Blimey," I thought whilst assessing the bleeding, "he must have severed one of the offshoot blood vessels from the tibial artery." I assumed that it couldn't be the tibial artery because he would have been dead by now. Still, I knew it was serious … very serious indeed. I applied loads of padding and pressure to the artery but, try as I might, I couldn't stop the bleeding and blood spurted everywhere. It left me with no option but to apply a tourniquet above the wound and then a large gauze dressing. After controlling the blood flow I then gave the soldier an injection of pain killer to ease the pain and help combat shock. I always carried a capsule of strong analgesia in my bag but had been given strict instructions to only use it in a dire crisis. As far as I was concerned this was one of those emergencies.

"Right medic, can I do anything to help?" asked the sergeant apprehensively.

"Yeah you can Sarge, he's definitely in a state of shock; can you get some blankets to wrap around his shoulders whilst I put a back splint on his leg." The back splint was shaped like a house troughing and fitted to the back of the leg to keep it immobile and comfortable.

"I'm with you lad, I'll go and get some now."

"Lad," I thought as he raced off to a tent, "he must be relenting towards me."

"There, he looks a lot better now." said the sergeant impatiently once I'd applied the splint and stabilized it with crepe bandages, "can we put him in the ambulance car now and get him back to Bamenda?"

"Just bear with me for a little while more please," I replied as I rummaged through my medical bag and took out a red indelible pen, "I've one more thing to do and it's very important." I then wrote 'T 3-15pm' on the soldier's forehead.

"What the flamin' 'eck is all that scribble about?" laughed the sergeant.

"You might laugh sarge, but this is really important. It is to remind me that I applied the tourniquet at 3-15, and that I have to release it every twenty minutes to allow the blood to flow; otherwise gangrene will set in. And it's not only to remind me; once we reach the hospital in Bamenda the medical officer and nursing staff will immediately be aware of the same once they see the 'scribble', as you call it."

"Good thinking medic, well done! Now can we get him into the stretcher Rover?"

"Right Sarge, he's ready to go now," I said once the patient was settled down on the canvas bed within the jeep, "just one favour to ask of you."

"What's that then?"

"Could you spare one of your lads to drive us back to camp so I can tend to Smithy on the way there ... I need to take care of the tourniquet? We should be there and back by tonight."

"No problem," he replied readily summoning one of his men. Within five minutes we were on our way.

On reaching Bamenda an emergency team was awaiting our arrival and everything went fine from thereon in. After filling in a report of the accident and having a bite to eat, the infantryman and I made our way back to the small outpost.

I'd no sooner got into my tent when Sergeant Jones approached me. "How's Smithy going on medic ... did you get him to the main camp all right?"

"Yeah Sarge, it was a bad break but he's in the best place now."

"He is that lad and all credit to you ... I put my hand up. I've been a bit hard on you but I won't mess you about any more, there'll be no more hassle from me ... you can take my word on it."

He not only honoured his word; he became quite matie towards me.

****

Most of the people who lived in these uplands were farmers and lived in small huts built of wood, clay and palm leaves. But some of the men were herders and these hardy men used to move from place to place and built light shelters from the use of poles and woven mats. It was intriguing to see them erect the flimsy refuges in which they passed the night. Next morning they'd be on their way herding cattle over rocky dusty terrain.

Just like the main camp the outstation employed native labour, and once again I made many new friends. The natives lived in outlying bush land huts scattered around our small outpost and they actually thought I was a doctor. On numerous occasions I treated the impoverished people for minor ailments and in some cases for serious injuries sustained in our employ. But I also used my nursing skills to help the families of these indigent people. I was committing an offence, but it seemed worth the risk, as these poor people had nothing and may have died without my help ... what was I supposed to do?

One time, Kumsala a small thin man in his early twenties came to see me with a worried look on his face. "Doctor John, you help me please ... my wife she is hurting."

"And where is she now Kumsala?" I asked sympathetically.

"She outside of tent Doctor John."

"Oh all right, bring her in here so I can have a look at her."

When he brought her inside I was a little taken aback, as she was only a slip of a girl and her left hand was swathed in a bloodstained piece of rag. She looked terrified, visibly shaking as she cupped the injured hand with her other and held them both close to her chest.

"Hello there, and what's your name then?" I asked gently, trying to calm her down.

"E-e-t-la!" she sobbed with tears rolling down her cheeks.

"Eeta," I queried.

"No no Doctor John," said Kumsala, "her name is Estella."

"Estella," I smiled, "that's a nice name ... what does it mean?"

"It mean 'Star of the sky' Doctor John," answered Kumsala.

"That's beautiful," I replied looking at the young girl, "and now my little star in the sky ... can I look at your hand? I won't hurt you." I detected a little response but she still cowered away from me like a frightened kitten.

"Ye-es, alright doctor John," she whimpered as a tear rolled down her cheek.

I carefully removed the soiled rag, but the young girl flinched as parts of it were stuck to the skin by dried blood. Eventually I exposed the wound, revealing a nasty laceration between her thumb and index finger. "Oh dear!" I thought. "This needs stitching and I've just promised her that I wouldn't hurt her." My concern stemmed from the fact that I didn't have any local anaesthetic in the tent.

"It bad Doctor John?" asked Kumsala rather concerned.

"Well it's not serious but it definitely needs at least five stitches. It's a nasty cut Kumsala, what happened?"

"Elephant grass Doctor John ... she cut hand on elephant grass."

"Elephant grass," I thought, "I should have known ... it's bloody lethal. The grass surrounding the outpost stood over six feet high and was very hardy with a razor sharp edge.

The young girl remained passive whilst I cleansed the wound but then came the hard part.

"Now listen to me Estella," I said soothingly trying to explain the procedure to her, "I know I promised I wouldn't hurt you, but now I have to do something to make you better, which will be painful ... do you understand?"

"Ye-es Doctor John," she whimpered, "I understand, you kind man ... I try to be brave."

I'd done plenty of suturing before but only on soldiers, never on a young girl like this ... I was more nervous than she was. I felt awful having to suture her hand without anaesthetic, unlike the time when I stitched Bullyboy's hand. Then again, he deserved the pain ... it was his comeuppance, and I hadn't felt any compassion for him at all. But in Estella's case I felt totally different ... my hands were shaking.

After cleansing the wound and spraying it with a special antiseptic lotion I managed to insert the first stitch right into the centre of the wound drawing the skin to a close, and then two more on either side spaced out equally. Up to this point she'd been very patient but then she became agitated and wouldn't tolerate any more.

As I attempted to apply a fourth suture she kicked and screamed and, even with the help of Kumsala, I couldn't possibly complete the task. She was only dainty but she had the strength of a tiger; I eventually had to give up.

"Ah well Estella," I said, "at least the skin has been pulled together, giving it a chance to regenerate ... it would never have healed as it was before."

"What is regenerate Doctor John?" asked Kumsala rather concerned.

"Oh it just means that the wound will heal better," I consoled him. "Anyway, I'm not a doctor Kumsala ... just call me John."

That's what I said but it didn't make a scrap of difference, as he politely replied, "Yes alright ... thank you very much Doctor John!"

I should have known better ... it reminded me of a similar reply that Kinton had given me back in Kumba.

After dressing the wound I gave instructions along with some cotton pads, a crepe bandage and some antibiotics.

"Kumsala ... Estella," I said as they left the tent, "don't forget to come back in ten days so I can remove the stitches."

I thought I'd seen the last of Estella but to my surprise she did come back ten days later and, happily, the skin had knitted together quite well, leaving a fine suture line.

Another time, Chimbu, a labourer, came to see me late at night and he was crying. "Doctor John, you come to my house please ... my boy very poorly!"

I gathered the First Aid kit and followed the gentleman about 500 yards into the undergrowth, arriving at a little mud hut. The inside was typical of all the other huts I'd been in and the little boy, about seven-years old, was lying on a single bed behind a sack curtain. Straightaway I could see the boy had some kind of fever, as he was sweating profusely. I did his observations to find his temperature was soaring at 105°f.

All I did was sponge him down and told his parents to encourage fluids.

"But he no eat or drink Doctor John," sobbed the mother who was frantic with worry, "we try all time but he eat nothing ... please no let our little boy die!"

"Listen to me," I said trying to console her, "the most important thing you can do for your boy at this moment is to get him to drink."

"But he no like water Doctor John," she sobbed all the more.

"Just wait here," I said as an idea came to my head, "I'll be back in twenty minutes."

"Yes Doctor John … we wait for you."

I went straight to the stores and bought two bottles of cordial, a blackcurrant and an orange juice. "This should do the trick," I thought, "it should be a luxury for the little boy."

When I got back to the hut the mother was still very anxious. "Doctor John, my boy, he no take water."

"It's all right dear, you leave it with me." The little boy, although drowsy, was still awake as I approached him. "Here sonny, try this," I said gently dabbing his lips with gauze, which I'd soaked in orange juice. He responded by licking his lips but then, after a while fell asleep … it wasn't a big response but at least it was something. Turning to the parents I tried to put them at ease. "Right, that's all I can do tonight, but when I'm gone I want you keep dabbing his lips like I did to keep them moist. Then mix some water with this fruit juice; I'm sure it will encourage him to drink. I'll be back tomorrow to see how he's getting on."

I did return the next day and the one after that and by then the little boy's temperature began to gradually fall, and thankfully, within a week it was almost back to normal.

"By 'eck!" I thought. "He looks a picture of health compared to the other night." Within a couple of days the boy was up and about and getting into loads of mischief.

The mother expressed her gratitude, making her feelings plain. "Thank you so much Doctor John, thank you … my boy he be fine now, thank you!"

"Whoa!" I said feeling embarrassed. "There's no need to thank me; you're the ones who have done the hard work, not me."

But the little lady wouldn't have it and continued to sing my praises. That's how it was. I continued to help the natives when in need and an affinity was formed between us … they made me feel like a king.

On entering the medical tent in the morning I'd find bottles of wine or other small tokens, on which someone had scribbled 'Thank you Doctor John'. Receiving gifts from these impoverished people, who had absolutely nothing, truly taught me the real meaning of life. Although I wasn't a doctor these humble people made me feel that I was making a difference. It was a wonderful uplifting experience, filling me with a feeling that I'd never had before, or since. The humble sensation dispelled any antagonism that may have previously been in my mind.

****

During my time spent at the outposts I had to do a couple of patrols and saw the odd propeller planes bombing various hillsides, but unlike when I was in Kumba, they were uneventful. Nevertheless, one patrol, which I was not attached to, went out on a mission from the Sante Coffee outpost after receiving reports of terrorist activity deep inside French territory. Awakened in the middle of the night a squad of soldiers set off under the command of Lieutenant Olsen, a fine upstanding officer. The dispatch had been of such detail that a back up patrol was sent along with them. One of the infantrymen in the second company, Alan Parkinson, gave a factual report of the incident when he returned to camp after the manoeuvre.

According to his account his platoon trekked for hours through dense bush land, finally coming to a ridge, which overlooked a valley overgrown with tall thick bamboos. It was amazing how the officers navigated their way through the thick jungle solely with the aid of a flimsy map and a compass. The lieutenant ordered most of the men to squat down on the spot whilst others surveyed the area. It soon became abundantly clear that they had stumbled upon a main terrorist camp.

"Right men," said the officer, "prepare yourselves, you know what's expected from each and every one of you. Synchronise your watches with mine ... we're going in at 05-00hours."

Most of the men felt frightened and butterflies built up in their stomachs, knowing full well that some may be killed in combat. Five o'clock came and into action they went, swarming down onto the camp, taking the terrorists completely by surprise ... the lieutenant's offensive was a total success. It was astounding just how smoothly the manoeuvre went with minimal casualties ... not one British soldier died, though some terrorists did.

231

The terrorists' camp was amazing in every respect. It was approximately fifty yards long, and stepped down on different levels of the bamboo-infested hillside. The roof of the camp was constructed from corrugated tin sheets, camouflaged by remnants of the natural surrounding vegetation. The design of the camp was fascinating, being self-sufficient, housing pens of stolen livestock, cows, horses, and poultry. There was a storeroom stocked up with provisions, beer and cigarettes. Another store contained an arsenal of weapons, but luckily for the British lads, they were old and antiquated from a bygone era. The infantrymen shuddered at the thought of what might have happened if the terrorists had been as well armed as themselves and aware they were coming. The terrorists truly were experts in camouflage … the French Air Force had been bombing the wrong hillsides for months.

Lieutenant Olsen did a good job and was deservedly awarded the Queen's Commendation for his action.

The lads celebrated their victory over a few beers, but within days the outpost settled down into its usual routine.

****

I got on well with Mick the cook, and we sometimes helped each other out. He did all the cooking in an old barn constructed with typical oak beams supporting the roof. I'd just carried some rations from the stockroom and he made me a mug of coffee. I was enjoying the brew when I heard some loud buzzing from above and felt some sawdust touch my face. When I looked up I was horrified to see some large beetle type creatures boring themselves into one of the large beams. They had red and yellow stripes like bees but were twice as big.

"What the bloody hell … let's get outa here Mick!" I panicked.

"Why, what's up?" he asked unconcerned.

"What's up? Just look up there at those bloody things!"

"Ha ha ha!" he scoffed. "They're just wood beetles that live in the beams … they're harmless."

"Harmless? They don't look bloody harmless to me the way they're boring into them beams … if they can go through solid oak that easy they must be lethal. Just look at the sawdust they're creating; they could make a right mess of us!"

He just cracked up laughing again, "You bloody crackpot John, they're not boring into the beams; they live in the knotholes and that's plain ordinary dust that they're scattering about with their wings ... it's not sawdust."

I calmed down a bit but wasn't entirely convinced; every time I looked up they looked awesome.

****

When the infantry mob were out on patrol, Mick not only had to do the cooking but had to do the washing up as well; if I wasn't too busy I would give him a hand. I didn't mind so much, but I used to finish up full of grease and there was nowhere proper to wash. The only facility was a small bamboo table that stood outside the tent, onto which we placed a bowl of cold water. We had to make do with this for both washing and shaving. That's what I thought until one evening I saw Mick going somewhere with a towel over his arm.

"Where are you going Mick?" I asked.

"I'm going for a bath ... where d'you think I'm going?"

"A bath ... what d'you mean, a bath?"

"I mean what I say ... a bath. Why don't you get your towel and come with me?"

"Too bloody true!" I blurted. "I haven't had a shower or a proper wash down in ages ... just give me a minute while I nip to the tent."

"Be quick then; I'm not hanging about."

I grabbed my towel and eagerly ran after him ... I couldn't wait. "Are you sure you know where you're going Mick?" I asked as he made his way through a patchy field.

"You'll see John, just follow me."

"Right, just give me a minute, I'm coming."

The field was choppy, on a slight slope and as we got to the bottom corner there it was enticing us to jump in.

"There, what did I tell you ... lovely isn't it?"

I couldn't believe it ... it was an old horse trough, full to the brim all right but there were loads of midges flying around moss, which floated on the surface of the dingy water.

"U-ugh! You're not bathing in that Mick surely to goodness?"

"I am that ... you please yourself what you do but I'm going to have a swill down, it looks like heaven to me." I watched as Mick scooped away the moss and then, standing up in the trough as naked as the day he was born, he started to sponge himself down. "Br-rr, this is cold but it's mighty refreshing," he laughed, "fifty times better than that bloody grease."

"I've got to admit Mick, it looks better now you've cleaned some o' that gunge from off the top."

"Go on John, give it a try," he said stepping out of the trough, "you'll feel tons better after."

"Oh why not, I've come this far I might as well go the full hog," I laughed now getting into the spirit of things. But as I stepped into the water it was so cold it made all my muscles tighten up. "Bloomin' 'eck it's absolutely freezing!" I moaned. I was in and out in fifty seconds flat.

"There, that wasn't so bad was it?" roared Mick in a fit of laughter. "I'll bet you feel loads better now."

"Yeah Mick, I've got to admit that after getting over the initial shock I feel great ... cheers!"

During the rest of my time at the outpost I joined Mick every night at the horse trough and was glad of it because, like he said, it was much better than going to bed stinking of sweat and grease.

****

I preferred working at the outpost to the main hospital in Bamenda and things worked out a treat for me because Mark, my working colleague, was more partial to working within the confines of the main camp. Nevertheless, I still had to do the odd duty within the encampment.

One weekend whilst I was there the CO put on a regimental parade and ordered every vehicle to be bulled up. It turned out to be a display of the camp's weaponry as a squad of infantrymen paraded around the camp in full battle gear behind lines of army vehicles. One Landrover towed a rather sophisticated cannon, whilst another displayed all the latest up to date radio equipment. After a small mock battle, we medics then put on a simple exhibition of First Aid on the so called casualties. It was all very impressive, but was nothing in comparison to what the local natives put on afterwards. Scores of ladies, dressed in the most colourful animal like costumes, danced merrily to the sound of jungle drums and primitive flutes. Wearing traditional decorative headgear, they pranced around displaying magnificent carvings made out of ebony, bone and ivory. The awesome ladies were then complemented by their menfolk, who romped and swayed about in Zulu attire, wielding a long spear in one hand and a large shield in the other. Every warrior was covered from head to toe in war paint, each in his own individual style. I thoroughly enjoyed the entire spectacle, and this was one time when the thought of a Zulu wielding a machete didn't put the wind up me.

****

One advantage of the main camp was that it was near a farm and the farmer rented out horses for a paltry one shilling a day. I was already well used to horse riding as, in my youth, my dad owned a mare named Peggy and he gave me the responsibility of attending to her needs. Besides mucking out the stable I groomed and fed her daily, and when she needed re-shodding I would proudly ride her bareback to the blacksmith's.

So now, when I was off duty I often went riding with one of my mates. Some of the horses were quite big but I never had any trouble controlling them. I usually started with a gentle trot, gradually breaking into a canter and finish up galloping around the disused racetrack. Some other lads were good riders too and we arranged races with side bets of cigarettes or cans of ale. I fared very well and my confidence grew to the point of becoming cocky … alas that was my undoing.

One day during one of the friendly bouts a teenage group of Arabs rode up on some majestic stallions. After watching the first race the young bunch broke out into a bout of laughter.

"What's so funny?" growled one of the soldiers.

"I tell you what be funny," replied a brawny lad, who appeared to be the leader of the gang, "you ride horses made for ladies."

"What are you on about?" I butted in. "These are good strong horses."

"Yes, they good, they strong for work on land, but no can run." the lad replied smarmily. "If you be fine rider, you try Arab horse … he fly like the wind."

At this the entire band of Arabs burst out laughing and started to chant, obviously trying to goad us into riding along with them. Needless to say their ploy worked … Rory, a Liverpudlian and I took the bait.

Right you're on," I said, "I'm for it."

"Yeah me too," said Rory, "just give me a horse and I'll show you."

That was it … within a minute I was sitting in the saddle clutching the reins of an Arab horse.

"By "eck Rory," I spluttered, "I've got to admit these are the most magnificent horses I've ever seen."

"Aye you're right there John, they have a different feel about them … they're so vibrant and lively."

"Right soldier boys," sniggered the Arab, "you ready; we go!"

Immediately the horses broke into a gallop heading for the open plain.

"Oh this is not too bad," I thought, "I can cope with this."

"Ha ha," Rory laughed making it plain he felt the same, "this is kid's play, it's easy peezy … if you can ride one horse you can ride 'em all."

That's what we both thought, but the young Arabs had other ideas. The ringleader suddenly let out a wailing sound and all the horses bolted, breaking into ultra speed. I enjoyed the thrill of the moment but after a few hundred yards fear started to creep in and I attempted to slow the horse down. But there was no chance … it had a mind of its own and was completely out of my control. I started to panic but strove to keep calm.

"Whoa boy, slow down," I shouted pulling tightly on the reins to no avail.

To make matters worse one of the gang rode alongside me and, in a fit of laughter, whipped the horse's backside. It didn't seem possible but the horse moved up another gear and now its feet weren't touching the ground. All the Arabs were racing at the same breakneck speed and thoroughly enjoying themselves … they truly were fine horsemen.

"Come on, pack it in," I pleaded to the leader, "you've made your point, now stop the flamin' horse … please!" But my pleas were ignored and I discovered the worst was yet to come. "Oh no!" I groaned as I saw a high stone wall looming towards me. The leading riders scoffed all the more as they floated effortlessly over the obstacle.

"Follow me soldier man," mocked the gang leader as he rode by, "this is good, no?"

As the wall loomed ever nearer the thought went through my head to bail off the horse but I was too scared to do that. "Come on John," I encouraged myself, "you can do this, just keep your nerve." I mustered up every bit of experience I could to negotiate the high jump; but it didn't do me any good because, despite my youthful experience with Peggy, I had never ever done any horse jumping before. By now the frisky stallion was primed up to take the wall and hell-bent on taking me with it.

"Oh well, here goes," I gulped as its front legs took off, "hang on John!" It took only a split second but as I was airborne, time seemed to stand still. However, my moment of flight came to an abrupt end as I was thrown from 'Pegasus', landing on the grassy plain and taking a few tumbles. I was shaken up but luckily didn't sustain any serious injury ... even so I did fracture my right thumb. As I sat there nursing my bruises Rory tapped me on the shoulder.

"Are you alright John?"

"Not too bad considering. I think I'll suffer tomorrow though ... how about you?"

"I'm alright, I bailed off when I saw that bloody wall coming up ... there was no way I was going to attempt that. I cringed when I saw you disappear over the top."

Just then the young Arabs returned. "Now you believe what I say?" smirked the henchman, "Arab horse is best in whole world ... no?"

"Yes I believe you, you creep," replied Rory."

"Yeah me too," I said holding my thumb, "and I've got this to prove it."

"You like I bring horses for you to ride back to camp?" laughed the young bloke.

"No thanks, we'll skip on that one," we both answered simultaneously.

As the Arabs rode off Rory and I picked ourselves up and limped back to base. We weren't too badly shaken by our experience... albeit a lot wiser. I found out later that the youngsters were from a clan, well-known around Bamenda for their fine horsemanship, called the Fulani tribe.

****

Whilst at the outpost I mated out with Neville, who skillfully went about his work in the Signal Corps. It intrigued me the way he tapped out messages in Morse code on a transmitter and I thought it was marvellous how he interpreted those dots and dashes. He was the main man in charge of communications between the main camp, our base and troops out on patrol.

"Blimey Nev," I said scratching my head, "how the bloomin' 'eck you can understand that bleeping is beyond me."

"It's easy once you get used to it John, it's made up of dots and dashes … I just tap quickly for a dot and slightly longer for a dash."

"Oh aye, I understand that, but it all comes through as a load of bleeps to me."

"Yeah it did to me at first, but after a while it clicked and now my ears are tuned into it."

"It still sounds like double Dutch to me."

"Neville just laughed, "Let's hope it sounds alright to them on t'other end of this wire eh! Anyway John, I'm off duty at twelve o'clock … do you fancy doing anything this afternoon?"

"I wouldn't mind going horseback riding … how about you?"

"That'd be great but there's a snag … some of the lads have already booked 'em."

"Bucked 'em Nev, how do you mean … like in a rodeo?"

"Booked 'em you silly sod … not bucked."

"Yeah alright," I chuckled, I was only joking. Anyway have you got owt in mind?"

"I have actually 'cos I heard two lads saying they got permission to borrow a Sterling machine gun each for a bit of target practice in the hills."

"You're joking, I didn't think that'd be allowed."

"No neither did I but there you have it …not only were they allowed but they each got a magazine full with twenty rounds."

"Well if that's the case I'm all for it … we can but try."

Sure enough, after some form filling, the munition's officer handed over two weapons, each with a full breach. Making sure the safety catches were on we set off with the guns slung over our shoulders. Heading for the hills we had to cross over a grassy plain and realised we were quite exposed to the elements.

238

"I'm not going to let off any rounds yet John," said Neville, "I feel quite vulnerable out here in all this open space ... you never know, we might need the ammo."

Neville's words must have been a prophecy because when we got within a hundred yards of the foothills a large pack of baboons confronted us. The leader was a huge fierce looking animal bearing its fangs and strutting about like a Zulu warrior protecting his tribe. In the background I could see infants clinging to the backs of their mother's necks. I'd never been as frightened in the whole of my life as I was at that moment, especially when the chieftain kept bolting forward in short bursts making threatening gestures. The incident back in Kumba, when Pete and I got chased with a native wielding a machete, was frightening enough ... but that happened so quickly that we didn't have time to think about it. But this time, Neville and I found ourselves in a waiting game, not knowing how the baboons were going to react.

"Bloody hell John," croaked Neville in a low shaky voice, belying his fear, "try not to upset the leader ... if he comes for us the rest of the pack'll follow him. Come on ... let's get out of here!"

"Yeah, don't worry yourself on that score Nev ... I want to get away from here as much as you do."

To add to the nasty situation, some of the baboons were coming round on our flanks. I felt the hackles stand up on the nape of my neck and my initial impulse was to take flight; however, my instinct told me to back off gradually.

Neville made it clear that he thought the same as I did, "Just back off slowly John ... don't run whatever you do or they'll have us."

"How about firing a shot into the air to frighten 'em off," I replied rivetted to the spot.

I don't know so much, it might work but then again it might trigger 'em off ... what with them having babies an' all."

So we cautiously backed off inch by inch praying it was the right thing to do, not daring to take our eyes off the encroaching baboons ... especially the ringleader, who remained menacing. Luckily for us, as we gradually edged further away from the pack, the baboons to our sides dispersed and made their way back towards the foothills. But the big one remained defiant, making a couple of extra lunges forward to demonstrate his dominance.

Grunting and growling through gritted teeth he sent off a clear message, "Get away from here and don't come back … this is my territory!"

Even after retreating a fair distance we still didn't feel safe.

"Bloody hell Nev!" I squirmed. "That was too close for comfort."

"You're not kidding John … I nearly wet myself."

"You nearly wet yourself … lucky you!"

"Ha ha, I know what you mean. Anyway, come on let's get the bloody hell out of here."

Later that night, whilst having a few cans of beer, we talked about our escapade only to be enlightened further about baboons.

"I'll tell you what lads," said a long-serving soldier, "I know a lot about baboons and their habitat … you don't realise just how lucky you were. They're strange looking creatures but they're very family orientated and, if you kick one they all limp."

"How do you mean?" I asked.

"I'll tell you what I mean … if you'd have fired a shot the leader would have attacked you, and even if you'd have killed him the others would have rounded on you and tore you limb from limb."

"What would they have done if we'd have set off at run?"

"Let's just say it's as well that you didn't … have you ever seen a dog stop in its tracks when a cat fronts up to it?"

"Yeah."

"Well, what happens if the cat decides to bolt for it?"

"I get you … the dog runs after it."

"That's right and that's exactly what the baboons would have done if you'd made a run for it."

"Bloody hell!" blurted Neville. "There must have been somebody up there looking over us."

"You can say that again Nev," I said making the sign of the cross, "we'll just have to put it down to experience eh!"

"Aye, an experience I don't want to go through again. Anyway, how about getting a few beers down our necks to celebrate."

"I'm with you there Nev … Cheers!"

We didn't even fire one round that day and I was never interested in borrowing any weapons after that.

****

I regularly had to go along with the infantry as they did official target practice and this is when I realised just how deadly accurate the SLRs were.

One day the sergeant major asked me if I wanted a go.

"Yes please!" I replied eagerly reaching for a rifle.

"Whoa soldier," he barked, "let's go over a few basic rules first! Have you ever fired an SLR before?"

"No Sir, but I was taught a few basic safety rules during our training at Queen Elizabeth Barracks."

"Basic rules!" he scoffed. "That's a damn sight different from firing one ... this is an SLR, the deadliest rifle in the world. Anyway, what are the main safety rules?"

"Check that the rifle is unloaded and that the safety pin is applied."

"Very good but also remove the magazine, then pull back the cocking handle, working it back and forth to make sure there's no rounds left in the breech. And do you know what SLR stands for?"

"Yes Sir," I answered feeling smug, "it's a self loading rifle ... accurate up to 2000 yards."

"Yeah and a lot further in proper hands. Anyway, don't feel so pleased with yourself just yet ... let's wait until you've fired a few rounds."

"Well," I thought, "I should be all right, I've won a few prizes back home on the fairground."

What a laugh ... it was like comparing a peashooter with a cannon.

The CSM had given me fair warning before I fired to hold the butt of the rifle tight into my shoulder but, to my cost, I didn't fully take notice of what he was saying.

"Bang!" The gun went off and the recoil had a kick like a mule, ramming the butt like a charging ram into my shoulder.

"O-oo-hh!" I cried out in pain.

"Serves you bloody well right for not taking heed!" he growled. "Now do it again, only this time, do it right!"

"O-oh, do I have to Sir ... I'd rather not."

"Get hold o' that rifle soldier!"

I didn't need telling twice, I could see he wasn't joking. This time I held it with all my strength but, being tensed up, it still hurt."

He wouldn't give up on me and insisted I fired off ten rounds. I improved somewhat but I was nowhere near the target. By the end of the exercise my shoulder felt as though it had been through a mangle, leaving it covered in telltale bruises.

"Bloody medics!" he rapped. "Give it us here and I'll show you how it's done."

He got down and fired, many rounds hitting the bull every time leaving me in no doubt that he was certainly a top marksman.

****

During my time spent in Africa the indigent people never failed to impress me. I'd worked alongside them in the field hospitals, bartered with them in the market places and we'd socialised together in bars, on the football field, swimming in the 'blue lagoon' and on many other occasions. I thought my emotions couldn't be stirred further until one very special day over the Easter period. It was Good Friday and I had a few hours off duty during the afternoon. I was walking near the market place when I noticed a crowd gathering.

Lots of residents were laughing and chanting and one of them greeted me, "Hello Mr John, you come with us, we go on procession ... it be very good." Before I knew it I was surrounded by lots of friendly natives.

"What procession?" I asked.

"Oh, 'tis wonderful Mr John ... it is the sorrow of Christ's passion."

"Yes Mr John," said another gleefully, "It is glory of Jesus' resurrection. You are our friend and we want you come with us ... you like very much."

"I feel honoured to be your guest," I replied humbly, "just show me the way."

I marvelled at the kindness and simplicity of these poor people, most of who lived in the foothills, as they pranced around in their finery on this special day. The women stood out in their brightly flower coloured dresses and headwear. The way to the church was hazardous with potholes and rocks and when we arrived it was already overflowing. Intermittent singing and music took place before and after the Stations of the Cross. What moved me most was that during the veneration of the cross, mothers held up their little ones to kiss the feet of Jesus. I later learnt that many of these good people had kept an overnight vigil in the church. To them the vigil was paramount to the central mystery of our salvation and many candidates were in readiness to be confirmed and baptised. After Mass the procession got underway and once again the path was treacherous. The lighting of fires, the cortege, the singing of the Exultet, the liturgy and the readings were just the prelude to something very special. Because when adults came forward for baptism and re-entered the church dressed in white garments, each one carrying a candle ... the jubilation of Easter broke forth. There was singing and ululating and people clapped to the rhythm of beating drums, whilst other danced alongside them.

"Come Mr John, you dance with us," laughed a few in unison, "you have plenty good time."

These friendly folk welcomed me into their midst with open arms, creating within me the most awe-inspiring feeling. The festivities went on for three hours and a feeling of joy and good spirit, accompanied by blissful songs and Gospel music, echoed around the peaks and valleys. All the merriment created by these friendly folk filled me with exhilaration.

As I laughed and chanted along with the happy crowd their simple expressions inspired me.

"You like Mr John ... it is good ... no?" asked a small fragile looking lady.

"It is very good, I like very much ... and you?"

"Oh yes ... the fire is like a light in my heart and the singing gives me wings ... I feel I can fly."

It wasn't just what she said but the way she expressed herself with so much simplicity. The festivities went on and on and before I knew it, it was time to go. Later as I made my way back to camp the celebrations, though not in full swing, were still ongoing. I couldn't help but think that despite the deprivation and being poor materially, these unique men and women had an undying deep rooted devoted faith.

"Where've you been John," asked one of the lads as I entered the tent, "we've had a right shindig in the NAAFI this afternoon with some of the infantry mob ... you missed a treat?"

"Oh I don't think so," I replied, "I've had a really fantastic day myself ... I wouldn't have missed it for the world." I then went on to tell him about it.

"Right," he quipped, "there'll be no need to say your prayers tonight then ... you'll have already said enough, e-eh."

I knew what he meant but I just smiled inwardly engrossed in my own thoughts, "That's where you're wrong my friend, I now feel that I need to pray even more ... those poor souls, struggling every day to make ends meet, put me to shame." They did as well ... they lived from hand to mouth not knowing where their next meal was coming from and yet they were so giving. To me they really were living the good life that God intended.

To finish the day off I had a couple of beers in the canteen with Neville and Mark. Needless to say I didn't need any rocking that night ... I fell asleep as soon as my head touched the pillow.

My last thoughts were, "U-um, what a memorable day that was!"

After the Easter period we all settled back down to the normal routine of army life. Time passed very quickly and before I knew it I'd only one month left to serve in the army. Subsequently, it came up on orders that I was to be transferred to the main camp in Buea prior to flying home.

CHAPTER SEVEN

THE LAST SIGHTING

Once again I found myself saying my goodbyes to special friends but on this occasion it was very sad. The natives got to know I was leaving and many came to see me off, some with tears in their eyes. They all gave me a hug as a gesture of friendship and each one said something like, "Goodbye Mr John I see you in Paradise … no matter how far apart, we will always be close together." Their humility was so touching.

Finally I bade farewell to Lucy and when I saw tears in her eyes, mine filled up as well.

"I'll always keep you in my prayers Lucy … God bless you!"

"And I keep you in mine Mr John … goodbye in this world I see you in the next." I hugged her tightly and she responded affectionately. It was a hard thing to do, but I finally had to tear myself apart, kissing her on both cheeks.

As I turned to leave I got a bit of a surprise … Paddy, the same driver who had brought me to Bamenda was waiting for me.

"Hello Paddy, I never expected to see you again."

"Aye well what it is … I get all the bad jobs." It was plain to see he hadn't lost his dry sense of humour.

"Oh yeah, I bet it broke your heart, having to leave Buea."

"You'll never know just how much. Anyway John, how did it go in Bamenda?"

"I've enjoyed it here; it was certainly a lot different to Kumba."

"Anywhere's better than that dingy sweaty hole."

"Oh I don't know so much; I've some good memories from there too."

"You must be the only one," he laughed. "Anyway let's be on our way."

"Will we get to Buea by tonight Paddy?"

"No way, I have to do a detour with some supplies ... we're going to stay at Mamfe tonight and then tomorrow night we're stopping at Kumba."

"Kumba, that's great ... I'll be able to see some of my old mates again."

"Does one of them happen to be Bill Hupboard," asked Paddy, "because we're picking him up to take to him to Beau with us."

"Yeah Bill's a good mate of mine, he was in the same intake as me back at Crookham."

"Oh that'll be the reason then; he'll be getting demobbed the same time as you won't he?"

"Yeah that's right Paddy. Anyway, did you say we're going to Mamfe first ... that's about ninety miles out of our way isn't it?"

"Aye it is but you know what the army's like ... you don't ask questions, you just follow orders."

"It's an Air Force base isn't it?"

"Too bloody true it is ... don't bloody mention it, I hate going there."

"Why what's up with Mamfe?"

"Oh it's not so much the place as the men of the blue brigade ... they're not what you can call the friendliest bunch o' guys in the world."

"Aye I've heard tales about them from some of the infantry lads; are they as unfriendly as what people say they are?"

"Well let's just say 'they're toffee nosed gits' and we'll leave it at that eh! Get your kitbag into the jeep, we've a long trip ahead of us and the roads are treacherous ... let's go."

I knew Paddy was right in what he said because we were now at the beginning of the monsoon season and we'd already had a couple of heavy downpours. In fact, a few days previously I got caught in an outburst whilst at the market. I was buying some last souvenirs when the heavens opened with large bolts of lightning flashing across the Savannah skyline. The deluge didn't last long, but it was enough to change the whole appearance of the place. As I trudged my way back up the mountain road to camp, small waterfalls cascaded down the grassy mountainside turning the road into slush. By the time I got back to base I was totally drenched.

Due to the road conditions it took seven hours to reach Mamfe and both Paddy and I were hungry and dirty. He was used to the routine and took us to a tent where we were bunked up with four friendly infantrymen. After dropping off the supplies and my kitbag all I wanted to do was have a wash and brush up.

"Thank goodness for that," I said, "I can't wait to get out of these clothes and have a shower."

"You'll be lucky," laughed Paddy, "the NAAFI and the shower rooms are out of bounds to army personnel."

"You're joking Paddy, where are we supposed to wash?"

"Over yonder in that compound," said one of the soldiers pointing to an old derelict building, "but you won't find any showers in there and you'll be lucky if there's any hot water."

"I don't believe this; how come we can't use the Air Force facilities?"

"Because like I said before John, they're toffee nosed gits," said Paddy, "I've driven to this camp umpteen times now and the brylcreem boys have always been the same; they seem to go out of their way to make things awkward for us army lads."

"But surely the NAAFI and the shower rooms belong to Her Majesty's Forces not just the RAF."

"You may be right. All I know is there's a big notice that says, 'RAF Personnel Only', and they stop any army bloke before he puts his foot on the doorstep."

"That's right," said one of the others, "and seeing as we're only passing through, there's not a right lot we can do about it."

"Well they can please themselves" I said arrogantly, throwing a towel over my shoulder, "because I'm gonna have a shower whether they like it or not."

"I don't think so John, you'll see," laughed Paddy.

"Maybe I will Paddy. There's one thing for sure … I'm gonna try."

"Good luck to you John," he laughed as I made my way towards the RAF station.

I could hear raised voices in the NAAFI but I slipped by them unnoticed into the shower room. The layout was certainly better than any of the army camps I'd come across and there was no one around. I'd just stripped down to my underpants when a bloke walked in.

"What are you doing in here, you're an army bloke aren't you?" he asked with a smarmy look on his face.

"I'm having a shower, what does it look like? And yes, I'm a medic and proud of it."

"But you can't use these facilities; have you not read the notice board?"

"Can't I? Just watch me," I replied arrogantly now completely naked and stepping into the shower. He didn't answer, but just turned around and walked away. "That was easy enough," I laughed to myself as the warm water gently eased my aching muscles, "I don't know why Paddy doesn't use these, they're superb." Everything seemed great, but then I heard voices and the clattering of boots on a concrete floor.

"Open up man!" a voice roared as a wooden batten rattled against the cubicle door.

I felt rather vulnerable but struggled to keep calm, answering, "Do you mind, I haven't finished yet."

"Open this door now you army lout or we'll break it down!" growled the voice angrily.

"Alright, steady on, I'm coming," I replied now feeling panicky.

"What the bloody hell do you think you're playing at you scumbag we don't want the likes of you around our quarters!" Under normal circumstances I would have retaliated but common sense prevailed, number one, I was stark naked and number two, there were three of them stood there wearing studded boots.

"Look lads," I said trying to placate them, "I've just brought a load of supplies to your camp today from Bamenda and I was absolutely knackered when I got here." I didn't know what ranks they were but they looked mean and menacing, and my little ploy had no effect on them.

They just stood there glaring at me for what seemed ages before one said derogatorily, "So you're a bloody medic are you?"

"That's right I ….."

"Shut your bloody mouth you maggot," he screeched, "just pick up your bloody rags and get out of here now!"

"Thank goodness for that," I thought as I attempted to put on my underpants.

"Medic!" screamed the ringleader. "Just pick them up I said and get out of here; you can put them on when you get outside."

"Right I'm going, I'm going," I spluttered as I gathered my meagre belongings. I was still wet and mumbled obscenities to myself, but was I glad to get out of that place.

"Mind the midgies don't bite," I could hear the thugs jeering in between fits of laughter as I hobbled away, struggling to put my clothes on.

"Bloomin' 'eck," I mumbled as I made my way back to our tent, "Paddy was right about them bastards; he won't half take the Mickey out of me when I get back."

He did too. "Ha ha, serves you bloody well right" he laughed. "Don't say I didn't give you fair warning."

Later that evening, seeing that we couldn't go to the NAAFI, we both made our way to a small outpost. It was getting dark and we could see a campfire burning and hear singing. When we got there it was the four infantrymen from our tent and they invited us to join them. They were good lads and we had a good laugh together, especially when Paddy told them of my escapade. I couldn't help but compare these friendly lads to the men in blue. I knew which group of men I would rather have had on my side in a crisis.

"How come those RAF louts are allowed to get away with it," I asked, "surely the NAAFI and the other facilities should be for us army lads as well?"

"Well what it is," replied one of the soldiers, "we, like you, are only passing through and there's only a few of us; whereas there's loads of them bloody mean bastards."

"Yeah, I see what you mean. I've got to admit that I'd heard rumours of them being an unfriendly bunch but now I know about it first hand."

"Aye bi jeebers you do," joked Paddy, "the whole naked truth … that's for sure."

"Ha ha ha," laughed the infantrymen in unison, "that's a good one Paddy; we like it!" The friendly banter continued until we heard some loud boisterous shouting.

"Oh no!" said one of the soldiers, "Corporal Bullyboy's back, that's mucked the rest of this evening up."

"Bullyboy," I thought, "surely it can't be the same Bullyboy who was at Kumba."

But sure enough, when I turned around, there he was. I couldn't believe it ... he was standing there as large as life, arrogantly shouting his mouth off and waving his arms about in the air in the same brash manner as when he left the courtroom back in Kumba. He cockily strutted about, brandishing a can of beer in one hand which was splashing all over the place.

"Bloomin' 'eck," I cringed, "I never thought I'd see him again. Just look at the big slob still using the same nasty tactics as when he was at Kumba; he doesn't look like there's any chance of him ever atoning for his foul deeds."

His big bulky frame tottered a bit, then he staggered towards me spouting in his usual foul offensive manner, "Get up you little arse'ole, you're sat in my place!"

I felt really intimidated, as I didn't want to move for the big hump of meat, but I didn't relish the position the thug had put me in. I visibly shook; he was a big man, and at this moment he looked gigantic.

When I didn't respond to his threatening behaviour his face contorted as he snarled, "Are you deaf or what you little git; move or I'll use you as a punch bag!"

"Oh, so your hand's healed has it?" I asked for want of something better to say.

"My hand?" he queried with a somewhat perplexed expression, "what the bloody hell are you talking about you little gobshite?" He approached me with clenched fist but then, lucky for me, a look of recognition came to his face. "By 'eck you're the medic who patched me up back in Kumba aren't you?"

"Yeah, that's me," I answered uneasily.

From that moment his whole demeanour completely changed. "Right medic, you really put me through some pain back then and I felt like bloody throttling you. But anyway, I've got to admit that you did a belting job stitching me up, my fingers healed up a treat ... cheers!"

"If only you knew of my intentions back in Kumba," I sniggered inwardly, "if I'd have had my way I would have stitched you up good and proper, that's for sure." I kept my thoughts to myself because I knew instinctively that his attitude towards me wouldn't have been quite so friendly if he knew the truth.

He seemed to be showing a nice side to his nature but then his true self came to the fore, as he started to boast about his so called conquest over the little native man back in Kumba and how he'd conned the army. But his bragging didn't last long because it soon became evident amongst the lads that they were repulsed by the atrocity. He actually offered to buy Paddy and me a drink but we refused. I was relieved at the outcome because common sense told me I was no match for this enormous guy, but I still felt annoyed for not having fronted up to him. Mind you, I was more disgruntled with the army for having allowed this beast of a man to carry on in his belligerent offensive manner.

Not to be put off by the distasteful man, Paddy and I enjoyed the rest of the evening.

"I'll tell you what Paddy," I said on the way back to the tent, "this has been one day I'll remember for a while to come."

"Aye, you're right there John, especially the men in blue eh."

"Ha ha, you can say that again."

The next morning, after a sparse breakfast, we climbed into the Landrover and headed for Kumba.

"How long will it take us to get there Paddy?" I asked inquisitively.

"You're one for questions aren't you? It'll take us as long as it takes ... we've got well over a hundred and forty miles to go and it's one 'eck of a bad road."

"Never mind Paddy," I laughed, "you can always shut your eyes."

"Ha ha, very funny ... it's a good one that because it's one o' mine."

I had to smile to myself; Paddy had a repartee second to none, no matter what I came out with he always had a spontaneous reply.

It had rained heavily during the night and as we travelled along the treacherous muddy road which had a steep drop on the passenger side, Paddy pulled up and pointed downward into a large gulley.

"Have a look down there John; you can just about make out the ruins of a Mammi wagon, which left the road at this spot during the last monsoon season. Sure enough, about a hundred feet below in the thick undergrowth I could make out an upturned vehicle with its wheels in the air.

"Bloomin' 'eck Paddy," I spluttered, "the poor bloke wouldn't have stood a chance would he?"

"Serves him right," he replied unsympathetically, "they drive like bloody maniacs and they don't seem to learn by their mistakes; I can show you plenty more wrecks along this road. It's only due to the skill of our Service Corps' drivers that none of our army trucks have finished up down there with 'em."

"But one of our lads did get killed," I said. "Word came through just before I left the *Devonshire* that a lad in the Royal Engineers advance party had left the road and ended up in an abyss below."

"Aye you're right there John, I forgot about that. But anyway, we got a right drilling when we first landed and were really put through our paces. At least our lads seemed to take heed from that accident, whereas the locals over here don't seem to learn at all and just blunder on regardless."

I had to agree with his reasoning, but I still couldn't help but feel sorry for the poor victims.

Luckily, the rain kept off and the sun shone brightly and we made steady progress. After travelling about seventy miles we stopped for a break and to cool off. As I sat by the side of a river with jungle foliage in the background, Paddy took a photograph of me, which I was to treasure over the coming years. After splashing my face in the refreshing water I climbed back into the jeep and we continued the final leg of our journey to Kumba.

That night I thoroughly enjoyed myself, celebrating along with my old mates, Rob, Pete, Bill, Rodney, Maurice and Spud Murphy and we exchanged a few experiences over a drink in the NAAFI. Apart from Bill Hupboard, this was the final meeting with my buddies, as all the others had enlisted into the army after me and still had a few months to serve.

"You jammy swine Johnny Cowell!" said a voice from behind me. "What are you having to drink?"

"Martin Grogan," I said without turning around, "I'll have a Tennant."

"You lucky sod, going back to England … I wish I was coming with you. Anyroad, don't forget to give my regards to the Burnley wallers when you get there."

"What are you moaning about, you've only got three months to do yourself haven't you?"

"Aye I know, but it seems like three years … I can't wait."

It was great kipping in the medics' hut once again amongst my old mates, talking of all the escapades we'd got up to.

"Do you remember when we put a lizard in Maurice's bed?" said Rob.

"Yeah you swines, but I got you all back," laughed Maurice.

"U-ug-gh did you!" I shuddered at the thought of the large black furry tarantula dropping onto my lap.

"What about New Year's Eve John," asked Spud Murphy, "I'll bet you remember that?"

"Do I; how could I forget that civilian's wife, she was absolutely gorgeous … I could have gone AWOL for her."

"Aye, I remember that well," laughed Rob, you were well sloshed."

"And I wasn't the only one … there were bodies flaking out all over the place, mine included. Boy, did I suffer for it next morning when I woke up under my mosquito net … I had the most ding-dong of all hangovers. I thought I was dying."

"Anyway John," laughed Pete, "how would you like a night out over the bridge on the French side, plenty of jig a jig an' all that?"

"Bloomin' 'eck, what a night that was … we'd have been slaughtered if the natives had caught us, especially the one with the machete. Still never mind eh Pete, we lived to tell the tale."

At that remark everybody in the hut burst out laughing.

"It's happen as well I didn't know about it at the time that you'd been over the river into the French Cameroons … I would have had to report it," said Spud Murphy trying to keep a straight face, "duty an' all that you know."

That's the way it was, fun and good humour, all taken in good spirit … I was glad to be going home and yet the moment was tinged with sadness. I'd only been out here in Africa for eight months but so many things had happened.

Next morning, Bill and I were up and ready to set off after breakfast. All our buddies waved us off with their usual wise cracks full of good humour as we passed through the gates.

"Don't let the QUARANCS get you down," they all shouted boisterously.

As I left Kumba for the last time my thoughts flashed back to when I first set eyes on the place, and strange as it may seem, it made me feel sad.

****

The last trek of the journey was rather bumpy but a few hours later we were driving through the gates of the main camp in Beua where I looked forward to meeting my old mates, Jimmy Mitchinson and Big Brian again. The camp itself was based on the slopes of Mount Cameroon, giving it a good vantage point over the outlying countryside. As I was shown to my quarters the first person I saw was Jimmy.

"Alright Jimmy," I said shaking his hand, "I hope you've been behaving yourself with them Quarancs."

"You must be joking," he smirked, "I wouldn't be seen dead with them."

"Chance would be a fine thing," I laughed.

"You can say that again," interrupted Big Brian as he entered the hut, "nice to see you again my old mate. Anyway, what's it like at Kumba?"

"It's alright if you don't mind sweltering your knackers off. Joking aside I enjoyed it there, especially working alongside the natives. Anyway, why do you ask?"

"Because I'm going there next week to serve my last two months out here."

"You'll be alright Bri ... honest! Once you get used to the mosquitoes, the crickets, all the creepy crawlies and the dense humidity you'll be fine."

"Thank you very much, that's all I need to hear."

"No, kidding aside Bri, I enjoyed it there. Anyway, how's Jean, your missus going on ... are you still in love?"

That remark triggered Jimmy off and he broke into a fit of laughter. "In love ... he is that! Ever since we landed here he's been like a lovesick teenager moping up and down all over the place."

Brian took it all in good fun, pouting his bottom lip and putting on the little boy lost look. "It's alright for you lot, but I'd only just got married when I got my calling up papers; you don't know what it's like."

The friendly ribbing would have finished at that, but then I broached him on something else. "By the way Bri, rumour has it that you've been made up to lance corporal … is it true?"

"That's a laugh," chirped in Jimmy, "he only had the tape for a week … the shortest serving lance corporal ever on record."

"Ha ha, very funny," snapped Brian.

"Come on then, fill me in," I said, "what happened?"

"You'll not believe it John," laughed Jimmy, "there was a lot of graffiti on the toilet walls and the CO had them re-plastered and painted."

"So, what's that got to do with Brian then?" I asked.

"Well, the silly sod went and scratched a message deep into the plaster with a rusty old nail saying, 'No more graffiti on this wall'."

"Nay Bri you didn't did you?" I said trying to keep a straight face.

"Alright, alright, that's enough piss taking for one session … any more and I'll sort you both out. Anyway, how about going to the NAAFI for a drink?"

"I can see things haven't changed much," I laughed, "right, c'mon then … let's go!"

On the way to the NAAFI Brian and Jimmy filled me in on some of their exploits whilst in Buea. They were attached to 'C' Company and lots of their patrols had been done using motorised boats to police the waters in the Delta region. Both had participated in incidents during which their platoon apprehended a few smugglers and terrorists.

The NAAFI Club in Buea was much bigger than the one in Kumba with more amenities … it even had a stage where the entertainment committee put on cabarets. I only had a couple of cans that night, as I was rather tired after my haphazard journey from Bamenda. But it was during this short spell that I was told a couple of interesting incidents, both of which involved Brian.

"Have you heard about Brian's episode when he had to go to a Nigerian court because of some stolen blankets John?" asked Jimmy.

"No I haven't," I replied, my ears pricking up, "but I'm sure you're gonna tell me."

"Hey that'll do," responded Brian, "that's all done and dusted … I'm innocent!"

"Oh come on Brian; let's hear it, it sounds interesting."

"Aye alright, but I'm telling the tale; you know what Jimmy's like, he'll get it all mixed up. Anyway, he only knows it from a second hand point of view."

"Oh yeah sure, I only went to court with you and watched the proceedings; it was a right laugh."

"Hey this is getting better all the time;" I said, "c'mon, let me in on it."

"Right said Brian, I'll tell it right from the start."

"Very good Bri, that's as good a place as any," laughed Jimmy devilishly.

After a good laugh, Brian started his short story. "About two months ago I got a job working in the stores and a right cushy number it was; no more patrols, it was great. Well I was working late one night and I heard some noise at the back of the hut so I went out to investigate. As I approached the wire perimeter fence I saw a young bloke on the other side of the fence carrying some sheets. I went closer to have a word with him, when suddenly a Nigerian policeman came out of the bush and nabbed the fella. When he saw me he automatically thought I was in league with the chap and asked me for my details. When I refused to give them to him he said he would report the matter to my superiors. He did just that and I had to appear in front of the CO the next morning. I protested saying I was only doing my duty because I thought something untoward was going on at the back of the stores."

"But surely Bri, if you'd have been involved the stock inside the stores would have been down wouldn't it?"

"That's what I said to the CO and so he ordered a stock check and they found that everything in the store was bob on."

"So how come you had to go to a Nigerian court," I asked.

"Well the local police said it was also a civil matter and they charged me."

"It was really funny what happened in the courtroom John," butted in Jimmy, "I nearly split my sides laughing."

256

"Alright Jimmy, I'm telling the tale," rapped Brian, "I don't need any help from you."

"Come on Bri, get on with it," I said now becoming a little impatient.

"Righto, here goes. Me and the young guy were in the dock and he was the first one to go into the witness box. Just like in England he had to swear an oath of truth, and this is the funny part. There was a bible, a blunderbuss and a bow and arrow, and he could choose any one to make the oath; he chose the bow and arrow."

"You're joking Bri," I laughed.

"No John, it's as true as I'm standing here; ask Jimmy if you don't believe me."

"It's true John; I told you it was funny."

"So how did you go on Bri; don't say you swore on the bow and arrow as well."

"Did I 'eck as like you silly sod; I swore on the bible."

"Right, so how did it finish up?"

"Well the young bloke got found guilty and was sentenced to three months hard labour, whereas they couldn't prove anything against me so I got off."

Jimmy and I laughed at that and carried on taking the Mickey out of him. I found the tale rather amusing as far as the blunderbuss and the bow and arrow were concerned, but I still felt sad for the local lad.

"Now tell him what happened when you had a day out with Spud Murphy," said Jimmy on a more serious note.

"Oh yeah, I forgot about that," replied Brian. "Spud was on detachment from Kumba and one day he asked me to go into town with him. We were strolling near the market when we saw a crowd of locals celebrating around a camp fire outside a rather large brick built bar."

"They seem to be enjoying themselves," said Spud, "let's go and join them." When they intermingled with the natives Brian realised they were drinking a white liquid that looked like milk.

"Don't be fooled by its appearance," said Spud, "that's Mimbo wine they're drinking and it's really potent; three of those will blow your head off."

"Mimbo wine; what's that?" asked Brian.

"Well I think it's made from coconut; it doesn't look up to much but it's quite good actually."

"Oh you've tried it then Spud I take it?"

"Brian when you're in a foreign country you should always try the local drink; how can you knock something if you don't try it out."

"Aye go on then, I'll just try a nip."

"Here you are Bri," quipped Spud as he handed him a tall glass of the intoxicating liquid, "get that down your throat."

"Ug-gh, it looks awful; it's thick like soup and it's got floaters in it."

He didn't like the look of it but surprisingly it tasted quite good. Consequently, after a couple of glasses the wine started to take effect and Brian felt like joining in the festivities. The locals were quietly dancing away to the sound of soft music but he started to bob up and down rather frivolously. Under normal circumstances this would have been quite acceptable but, unbeknown to Bri and Spud, this situation was totally different. Brian was thoroughly enjoying the moment until an official came up to him and asked him to be more respectful, as this was a funeral. Brian was really embarrassed and felt like crawling under a stone: he couldn't apologise enough. The official read the situation well and was very understanding and told them they were welcome to stay for the proceedings.

None of the locals took offence because they seemed to know that Brian was unaware of the circumstances. They stayed a little longer and then Brian needed to go to the toilet. On making enquires he was told to go through the building to the outer back. As he walked through a long bar he had to pass through a backroom that was lit with a Tilley lamp. As he passed through the small room he couldn't believe his eyes for there, laid out on the floor on top of a coconut type rug, was an elderly lady embalmed totally with flowers and large palm leaves, with just her face showing. As he gazed down at the lady he could hear knocking from the outside and on leaving the hut, two men were chipping away at a large tree trunk and carving it out to the shape of a boat; it was to be the poor lady's coffin. On passing the lady on his way back through the bar he quietly paid his respects by making the sign of the cross.

"Bloomin' 'eck, I never expected that," he said after telling Spud what had happened, "that was some experience."

Spud just smiled, "I never said anything but I kind of expected something like that; I've seen the likes of it before in other countries."

After Brian finished his tale I was struck again by their beautiful culture: a culture that never failed to amaze me.

It was Jimmy's and my last night in Africa so we decided to enjoy it. As I entered I could hear lots of laughter and the star turn was no other than Clowney the gifted man who won the talent competition back on the *Devonshire*, and he was now Corporal Clowney. He really did have a special talent and he had every one of us in stitches. His special magic wasn't just restricted to entertainment either … he had a God given, genuine unselfish gift for creating happiness, not just amongst the soldiers but the local inhabitants as well. This came to light the following morning when I, along with my friends, was preparing to leave the camp. When I left Bamenda I got a good send off but nothing like the one that the locals of Buea gave to Clowney. At least a hundred natives turned out to see him off, thumping drums and playing other musical instruments. They formed two lines so he had to pass through a passageway of natives and as he walked the gauntlet, ladies festooned him with garlands of flowers and threw their arms around his neck and kissed him.

I couldn't help but compare the difference with Corporal Clowney and Corporal Bullyboy. The contrast was from one extreme to the other … one was so full of love and one so full of hate. These indigent people openly expressed their love and gratitude towards Clowney, and as I looked at this special gentleman it was plain to see which of the two men was truly the happiest.

****

The hour had finally arrived for us to depart. Just like the day we arrived, the form of transport was a 3ton Bedford truck, which joined others to form a convoy. As friends waved us off I looked back in nostalgia, wondering if I would ever see any of these wonderful people again. I'd only been in the Cameroons for nine months but it had certainly won me over.

As the truck drove through the camp gates I started to reminisce about meeting the Kumba natives for the first time ... George, Alphonso, Dominic, Nelson, Matthias, Kinton ... not forgetting our tent boy, Pius Tashi. All the fine times and the leg pulling amongst my peers, the table tennis when Mark Radiven and I competed against the European businessmen, the basketball game when Martin got three days' jankers, the gymnastics, but most of all, the football match against the brave barefooted Cameroon players. I even pondered on the time I got seven days' jankers for a paltry offence, whereas Corporal Bully Boy got off scot free for a vicious attack on the poor native. My final reflection was of the Blue Lagoon, and I couldn't help but wonder how the little boy, who I had pulled out of the lake, was prospering, knowing full well that it was highly unlikely that I would ever set eyes on him again.

"Are you alright John?" asked Jimmy Mitchinson. "You're daydreaming again."

"Yeah, alright Jim, I'm just reflecting on the good times I've had out here in Africa."

"Oh aye ... do you fancy stopping then?"

"No not really," I laughed, "I'm looking forward to going home but somehow it all seems so sad."

"U-um, I know what you mean, but think of all the hard times as well ... the torrential downpours during the monsoon season, trudging about up to our eyeballs in mud, not forgetting the night patrols and getting cut to ribbons on elephant grass."

"OK Jim you've made your point. I really do want to go home ... honest!"

The trucks made their way through dense jungle country, but didn't head for the same bay where the *Devonshire* had docked, as on this occasion, the army had made arrangements to fly us home. We eventually ended up by the side of a typical jungle river where three large barges awaited to transport us to the airport. The barges were anchored to a small wooden jetty surrounded by mangrove and the thick undergrowth almost concealed the boats.

"Blimey John!" said Jimmy. "I hope there are no crocs hanging about in that water."

"Of course there be crocodiles in mangrove," scoffed an African guide, "the dense thicket be ideal habitat for them and there be plenty snakes as well."

"Right Jim, that answers your question, "I laughed, "do you feel better now?"

"Get lost John!" he replied spontaneously. "Never mind, we should be alright once we're aboard."

As the barges sailed up river the sun came out displaying a vivid blue sky. A happy mood descended giving us all a feeling of wellbeing, especially when we stripped off down to our shorts so as to top up our tans for the last time. Further upstream the river converged with other confluencing streams and gradually became so wide it compared to the River Nile. Every now and again we passed little hamlets and could plainly see natives on the riverbanks bathing themselves in the cool water as naked as the day they were born ... including men and ladies together.

After chugging along at a slow rate of knots for a few hours I set eyes on the most beautiful scenery I had ever seen in my life ... no artist could possibly have caught its splendour. Even as a little boy I'd always been an outdoor person and a nature lover, but this was far beyond my expectations. Beyond the thick green lush jungle, standing proudly in the background silhouetted against a vivid red sky, was a majestic snowcapped mountain, and a glorious sunset reflected its image in the deep water. I knew at that moment I would never ever see anything more beautiful ... I thought I was in heaven. I felt so uplifted that once again I drifted back into a nostalgic state.

This time my memories were of Bamenda. The kind impoverished people who would give their last penny, the bartering in the market place and how they used to hail me and call me Doctor John. The warm friendships I had formed with the native workers, especially Lucy. I smiled to myself when I thought of my escapade with the Arab horses, and the scary episode my friend Neville and I had with the baboons. Finally I thought of all the friends I had left behind. My time spent in the Cameroons had certainly been different and I wouldn't have missed it for the world.

"Hey John, look at them over there," said Jimmy bringing me back to reality once again.

"What … where Jimmy?"

"Over there in them barges … they must be our replacements, who've just been flown in from England … they're as white as ghosts."

As I looked across the water I saw three barges loaded with troops, sailing close to our boat in the opposite direction.

Bloomin' 'eck," I laughed, "were we that white when we arrived, they're like sheets."

All the troops on our boat started to cheer and exchange friendly gestures, "Alright lads, have you been bathing yourselves in Persil or what?" "Go on, get in there and keep our end up, show them bloody French troops what you're made of."

"Now's your chance John," joked Jimmy, "if you still want to stay … dive in and swim across now and join that lot."

"Ha ha, very funny … anyway, it's too late they're nearly past us."

"Yeah righto, but do you know something, we can't be all that far from landing now 'cos it's obvious that those soldiers haven't had any sun on their backs."

"Aye, you could be right there Jimmy."

Sure enough, within twenty minutes we pulled into a small docking area at the mouth of the Mungo River. The small port was in Dualle, the capital of the French Cameroons, where French army wagons were awaiting our arrival to transport us to the airport. The last leg of our land journey took about forty-five minutes and all the men cheered when they saw our plane, a Bristol Britannia, being refuelled on the concrete runway. I was quite excited despite feeling a little apprehensive, not ever having flown before. Excitement reached its peak as we all converged in the airport bar for a celebratory drink. It put me in mind of when we were on the *Devonshire*, but this time there was no reason to be anxious. To add to the occasion, another medic, Johnny Church, joined us and we spent the next hour singing and rejoicing. Sadly, all good things come to an end.

That's it," said Jimmy, "as a voice came over the loudspeaker, instructing us to go to our boarding gate, "come on lads, let's go … it's time to go home."

It was a great feeling, especially when three gorgeous airhostesses greeted us as we boarded the plane. To top it all the ravishing ladies waited upon us hand and foot and treated us like kings. We'd just got settled when the captain announced that the flight would be in two stages and we would first be landing in Tripoli, Libya for a three-hour stop. Cheers resounded around the plane at the thought of another drinking session. It was good really because once we reached Tripoli it gave us a little more time to say goodbye to our friends. My stomach felt a bit wheezy as I experienced my first ever landing but it settled quickly after we disembarked.

Despite the late hour it was bright, as a full moon lit up a clear night sky displaying yet another beautiful scene. We were all one big happy family as we drank, sang and laughed in a luxurious lounge overlooking the airport and beyond. As we sat there watching the planes come and go, some chatted about their exploits whilst others broke into song as they got merrier and merrier.

"E-eh, this is grand," said Jimmy as he took a sip of ice cool lager, "I could stand this forever."

"Aye it is Jim," I responded by raising my glass. "Cheers to the Cameroons!"

"Cheers John! I'll tell you something for nowt, I never thought that I'd ever be here in Tripoli … it puts me in mind of that war film that John Wayne was in."

"Yeah I know the one you mean, I think it was called *Sands Of Iwo Jima* … he played the part of Sergeant Stryker who, along with some raw recruits, took the island under a barrage of Japanese fire, only to be shot in the back by a sniper."

"Aye, that's right, it was a bloody great film … he was nominated for an Oscar wasn't he?" hicupped Jimmy.

"Aye tha's right. The theme tune went, *From the holes of Monte Zuma to the shores of Tripoli,* or something like that."

"Well whatever you say. Here's to John Wayne."

"Cheers Jimmy. You know something; I never thought I'd ever get the chance to go abroad either. You've got to admit, that's one good thing about army life."

"Aye I suppose you're right. Anyway, here's to it," he hicupped again, raising his glass once more. "Cheers!"

Shortly after, we boarded the plane and yet again the beautiful hostesses treated us like gentry. The beer and the atmosphere started to take effect and I fell asleep only to wake up as we were landing at Stanstead Airport in London. Looking out of the window I thought I was in a different world as it was misty and raining.

"Ah well, back to reality," I mumbled to myself.

After passing through customs we boarded a coach that took us to Euston Station. It was just as well that we had said our goodbyes back in Tripoli, as once we disembarked everybody dispersed very quickly, all eager to catch their connections home. Nevertheless, Jimmy and I managed to see Johnny Church off as he caught his train to Liverpool.

"Well, I've another hour to wait before my train leaves for Wigan," said Jimmy, how about you John?"

"You're lucky, mine doesn't leave for another three hours yet. Anyway, do you fancy going in that café over yonder for a brew?"

"Aye, why not? I could do with taking something for this hangover ... I feel as though my head's gonna burst."

"How about going in a bar then," I laughed, "the hair of the dog as Spud Murphy used to say."

"U-ugh, no thank you! I couldn't stomach any beer at this moment ... just the thought of it makes me want to puke."

"Righto, to the café then for a couple of strong coffees."

We had our last laugh together over a brew and a good old English breakfast before walking to the platform and shaking hands.

"Well John lad that was some experience out there in the Cameroons wasn't it?"

"It certainly was Jimmy ... and all the better for having good mates."

"Ah well I'll have to go," he said as the platform porter started to check the carriage doors, " I'll see you in two weeks time back in Crookham when we get demobbed ... have a good leave."

"Right Jimmy, the same to you ...see you later, safe journey."

****

As the train pulled out of the station I stood there all alone with just my kitbag for company. It seemed strange as a mixture of emotions, ranging from feeling sad, melancholic, nostalgic to sheer happiness, overcame me. There I was, aged just twenty-two in the prime of my life with money in my pocket, and I was going home to my beloved family and friends. I'd bought presents for my brothers and sisters and a special one for Mum and couldn't wait to see their faces. I looked at the station clock and noted that it was approximately thirty hours since we left Beau, "Ah well John lad," I smiled to myself taking a deep breath, "the weather might not be so good but count your blessings; you've got a lot going for you."

With that in mind I picked up my kitbag, threw it over my shoulder, stuck out my chest and proudly strutted to the train. As I sat on the train watching the green fields pass by I marvelled at the simplicity of the way the Cameroonians lived, and I felt proud to have witnessed life in its purest form. I was going home, feeling much more enriched than before my venture in the Cameroons.

****

EPILOGUE

When I left Africa, the King's Own Borderers were replaced by the First Battalion of Grenadier Guards. Suspected terrorists captured by the British infantrymen during my service in the Cameroons were approximately 240, of which about a third turned out to be known terrorists. After the plebiscite the Southern Cameroons and the French Cameroons united together under one Government to become the 'Cameroon Republic' under the leadership of Prime Minister, Ahmadou Ahidjo. At the same time, Northern Cameroons joined Nigeria.

****

It felt good to go home to a warm welcome by my two brothers and three sisters, not forgetting Mum. One thing that took me by surprise was how much my youngest sister, Barbara, had changed. When I left just ten months previously she was just a slip of a girl, but in such a short time she had blossomed into a beautiful young lady ... and I told her so. During my leave I enjoyed going out to places where I could show off my tan, especially the swimming baths. I couldn't contact my mates, as they were all in the Forces so I spent most of my leisure time with my brothers.

The ten days on leave passed quickly and before I knew it I was on the train making my way to Queen Elizabeth Barracks in Crookham where I met up with my comrades Jimmy Mitchinson, Bill Hupboard and Johnny Church to complete my final week prior to being discharged. We had a few nights out on the town and during the day we mainly lazed about. We all learnt to be expert skivers and each one of us always carried a sheet of paper in our hands as though it was an important document. Thus, if a sergeant or any high-ranking officer saw us it appeared as though we had an assignment. After the hectic time in the Cameroons the days at Crookham passed slowly, but eventually the day of demobilisation arrived.

We all took the same train to London and once again said our goodbyes. But on this occasion it was different because we all knew it was very unlikely that we would ever cross paths again. Just like the previous time, Jimmy and I were the last to board our trains. That day, forty-six years ago, was July 13th 1961, and I have never set eyes on him since. Jimmy was a special friend and I have been to Wigan many times on my travels but I have never been able to contact him. His address was 8 Afghan Street, Wigan, but in spite of having this information my search always came to a dead end. The first time I sought him out was approximately twenty years later but Afghan Street had been demolished in the name of progress. Once, whilst on Wigan Pier, I went through the telephone directory and called up every Mitchinson in the book, but to no avail.

I have however kept in contact with Big Brian from Leeds ... and even now he still frequently visits me. Then just recently, out of the blue, I got a phone call off Robert McNaughton, from Halesowen, who'd obtained my name and telephone number from the Internet. Between us we arranged a reunion with Brian, and together with our wives and lady friends, we had a night out in Burnley. It was the first time we'd all been together in forty-three years, and it went down a treat.

I've bumped into my Burnley mates on odd occasions and chatted about our African exploits. But when I first saw Martin since leaving Kumba he told me something that made me feel green with envy. Unlike me he, along with other troops, sailed home on the *Devonshire* and the lucky blighters got some shore leave on Gran Canarias, one of the Canary Islands.

"It was bloody great John, you missed a treat ... the young señoritas were absolutely gorgeous," he bragged rubbing salt in my wounds.

Shortly after returning to 'Civvy Street' I started courting with the girl Edna Simpson, whom I'd met on the night out with Martin whilst on Embarkation leave before going to Africa. We were married exactly two years later on the same date as I got demobbed; incidentally, Big Bri and his wife Jean came over from Leeds to attend my wedding. I started to work in the building trade and within three years my first son, John, was born and two years later Craig arrived on the scene. Money was tight at first but after some careful thought I undertook a Government training course where I worked alongside two new-found friends, Steve Burke and Roger Davey. On completing the curriculum I got a job as a shopfitter, working the length and breadth of England, Scotland and Wales. The hours were long but the pay was excellent, quashing any money problems. I later started my own joinery business and worked hand in glove with Steve, taking on contract work. I did fairly well and at the age of thirty-eight I went into the nursing profession and qualified as a state registered nurse, working on various departments including the 'Accident and Emergency.'

I retired at the age of fifty-five, which gave me the opportunity to write my first book, a biography of my mother's life: *The Broken Biscuit*. I then went on to write my autobiography … *Cracks in the Ceiling*, and finally decided to record my personal memoirs of army life in the Cameroons. It took me quite a while to come up with a title, but with some help from my ladyfriend I finally settled for *Elephant Grass*.

Just recently in May six Cameroon friends from Liverpool, Leeds, Birmingham and Burnley visited my home where we spent a pleasant afternoon chatting about our little adventure in Africa.

Whenever in life I am feeling at a low ebb I always think of those wonderful people in the Cameroons, it never fails to lift my spirit and I count my blessings. God bless the Cameroonians!
****

Incidentally, about twenty years after being demobbed from the army, something catastrophic happened in the Cameroons. Due to volcanic activity over millions of years, an abundance of toxic gas had built up underneath one of the large lakes and laid there dormant, trapped by thick layers of limestone. The area was not renowned for being dangerous so the authorities were unaware of the hazardous substance lying below the surface. Then sadly, one fateful night there was a small earth tremor. It was only slight on the Richter scale and didn't cause much concern. Be that as it may, the quake was enough to create a minute crack in the limestone, allowing deadly toxins to escape. Chemical reactions took place as it seeped upward through the water and mixed with the open air. Breezes then carried the deadly poison through the atmosphere, enveloping villages for miles around. Sadly, next morning, thousands of inhabitants were found dead in their beds.

When I heard the news on television it sent a shiver down my spine. I often wonder if Lucy, Pius Tashi, the little boy I pulled out of the lake, or any of my other friends survived … I can only hope.

One day, God willing, I would sincerely love to visit Kumba and Bamenda for old time's sake.

****

SYNOPSIS

Elephant grass is a tale of a young man's exploits in the British Cameroons, West Africa, during National Service in Her Majesty's Forces. John was raised amongst the abject poverty of the 1940's during the era of the cotton mills, clogs and shawls, and the knocker-up. His stint in Africa opened his eyes, as the impoverished people were poor beyond compare. Despite living in dire circumstances, the indigent people would gladly give the clothes off their back to help others, and their friendship was second to none.

The story starts in Plymouth, Devon where John was a nursing orderly in the Royal Army Medical Corps, but really gets going on the *Devonshire,* a large troop ship taking seven hundred troops to the Cameroons to restore order during a plebiscite. After many years under the oppressive regime of Nigeria, the British Cameroons was seeking its independence. There had been recent uprisings in neighbouring countries, namely the Belgian Congo, and so trouble was rife in the region. Like all conscripted men, John had to put up with the constant bawling of all the NCOs' foul language, ranging from the lance corporals through to the regimental sergeant majors.

Despite going to a war zone, the troops enjoyed a two-week ocean voyage, treating it more like a cruise. Deck competitions, concerts, drinking, and fun games were all part and parcel of keeping the men's morale high.

On reaching the British Cameroons in West Africa the main task force set up camp at Buea close to the coast at the base of Mount Cameroon. John was first posted to Kumba, a camp fifty miles inland in the middle of thick jungle country that was rife with mosquitoes. This part of the world was clammy and humid and renowned as 'the Whiteman's Grave. He was later transferred to Bamenda, a further one hundred and fifty miles north into mountainous countryside where the air was much fresher and easier to breathe.

Working in field hospitals or going out on patrols alongside twenty-three troops and a local native tracker to combat terrorism became an everyday practice. John struck up a strong affinity with the local inhabitants which created many interesting incidents. It is also a tale of camaraderie between his fellow soldiers through good and bad times. He gets up to many antics, and sometimes finds himself in dicey situations, but somehow overcomes them. Despite many setbacks he comes through with a smile on his face, feeling much more enriched due to his African experience.

It is a story of wit, humour, compassion and love for our fellow man. Most of all it depicts that in spite of adversity, the human spirit can rise to great heights.

****